SIX MONTHS' HACKING

or,

Six Years Hacking
Six Months Aint No Sentence

John M. Bennett Hacks Jim Leftwich's
Six Months Aint no Sentence
2011-2016

&

Other Mysteries

Including input from Iván Argüelles, El Inca Garcilaso de la Vega, Samuel Beckett, *Ritos y Tradiciones de Huarochirí*, *The Aldine Speller*, Felipe Guamán Poma de Ayala, Juana de Ibarbourou, Scott MacLeod, Seckatary Hawkins, H. P. Lovecraft, Paul Valéry, Vsevolod Nekrasov, Stéphan Mallarmé, César Vallejo, William S. Burroughs, José-María de Heredia, José María Heredia, *El Libro de Chilam Balam de Chumayel y de Tizimin*, Juan L. Ortiz, Homer, Raymond Queneau, Omar Viñole, José Lezama Lima, Michael Dec, Benjamin Péret, John Crouse, Bernardo de Balbuena, Pétrus Borel, José Antonio Ramos Sucre, Antonin Artaud, Vicente Huidobro, Tristan Tzara, Frédérique Guétat-Liviani, Olchar E. Lindsann, Bill Beamer, Peter Sherburn-Zimmer, Théophile Gautier, Diane Keys, and others.

LUNA BISONTE PRODS
2021

SIX MONTHS' HACKING or Six Years Hacking
Jim Leftwich's Six Months Aint No Sentence

Some of these poems have appeared in the following excellent venues:
Otolliths, inAppropiateD pRess, KART, On Barcelona, Gritty Silk,
Experiential-Experimental-Literature, Degu: A Journal of Signs,
Altered Scale, Thrice Fiction, Naked Sunfish, DOC(K)S, Pense Aqui,
Truck, Word For/Word, Utsanga, in several books by John M. Bennett,
on various electronic blogs and such, and perhaps in other places which
my frailties have been unable to identify. - *JMB*

Book design by C. Mehrl Bennett

ISBN 9781938521775

https://www.lulu.com/spotlight/lunabisonteprods

```
  *  *  *
  *  *  *
  *  *  *
  *  *  *
  ****
  / o \
  LBP
```
LUNA BISONTE PRODS
137 Leland Ave.
Columbus, OH 43214 usa

CONTENTS

ILLEG

amei hou toh eye ear ser pents sen
ato paper stockyards sif grit saw
debt run demonst graff release
skull ro undi tearg res ista
sweaty rattle market cor
pse unconsciou bail
out movem meat c
ops g ras jac
ctur war h
ours nuc

mask

gnosis s
teak knot
world erasure
midd le loaf the
weak lunch prank occ
vacant cannons swarm re
occupy liber eggs educ storm
ponzi nothing concave ambience
rotates prisor thematic hanc actions
liquid cameras egg technique obscu bawa

GHOST

John M. Bennett after Jim Leftwich's
Six Months Aint No Sentence, Book 12

DROVE

trance act bread the
tribe gut]garage[
flux gun horize soci
lashing
roof unwante telep city
social strate feed
back
problematizes trolley luggage
escape spoon history soar
damp ears breach space
garden hotel death ash
trays feast global sur
veillance photog
eye voice neith
shovel anti
thesis razor
)glitter(,beak
pie debar war theory balloon
hamster
drool
nouvea lan
guage st raws reel
the ersatz ear-clock
turn tactic
the mountain heart the
fugue divi sink
bodies
egg
prax contra fungus commerce

impossible mult cir
cular bacon
a not
S
arsenal pepper
N
mea streets
organ books
pages prog ot

2

her c age
o me
tal
)then have(
co agulate
tooths rep conceptualis en
try cult
burial dreams
garbage ,pool ka
popu cobble ego
tism ,o pen literat
snow
steak
maga
)fert(
cente journe
devoted cur up fork suit
cake works ,vocal what time
journa Tower family
killed
teleph
shadowy cooking table
armada lagoon ,snakes
lettrim bags con

crete gas station
hinge information)war(
scena rejecti documentat
eve
visitor
intole ,public soup ,isla
soeuv ,wake ,rugs
writing pools
completes Santa trag water
birds
bus
worlds

Through Jim Leftwich's Six Months Aint No Sentence Book 9

INFEX

himaso prior week even
hur now
corrosion lang cit
tlin huts sea
tues wee dema night
thinks each cloth
aerosol practic ladder
sleeves fork toll mot
icos duck
irgin gloves con saus
age glints crick
et soup vulg
ity uture c
oil hax funnel
smeg rive ha
violer milk crate
socks sor sky
bean rights solu
ooth anal cours ox
cop butt
corn flood balls
gnaw
ethic
flags
burgers
))ddoubble ttoorr((

Found in Jim Leftwich's
Six Months Aint No Sentence, Book 13
Dec. 23, 2011

POSTPREOCCUPATION

exterior socks the
X buried em
bedding the
drainage pipe
book corpus and
dung elite
drugs horro the
desk films
bawa sea
skin stu
pond horizon
forc militan the
weakness valve
micro poet fields
bees the
blurr unint
23 cat bubbles
solio ider eel
corridors
stock tube thoughts
blak sex protest
radia
radica
organ bailouts leg
poir trans sky
comb strike
hoarding
damage oil
nothing
knot
oc

3

seas
hair
prot toe
surveillano erotic muth
neck flake
dream
sea
beat
sky vipers
hungry address
hose floor
anvil
meat
bean
horse suits
huma blur paradig
feathers
feral ouch forks
histo
rooftop
murde docum
fire eggs and guardia
uranium enigma moving
plaza aboliti
plagia
cheap produc
viral parado fantas
agenda
lizards
febrile capita gecko heat

3

banks wake
died
inertia
knee
Aztec crossing
productivity
worms
splendid nadir
flat
chicken
polic
gnaw mask
gloves theories
impulses
soap
war grain
tranc beauty
insects
poets
brain legs
boundary rat
horrors fought deeply
generate
absurd
frogs
peel
wash
occup
oc oc
up

After Jim Leftwich's
Six Months Aint no Sentence, Book 11

OPTICAL CUP

optical lack each
america houses
self automobile

corpse
left
together

birdseed exposure

wordsworth bulges
topsoil
nibbled owners

map noise
noise eye

fascist history

variation
what

joke body

become explosion

this
face

un
wat
wake

neter volts

erectile story

dandruff
right
the raft erases
mesiter civil

trucks
aspic volcano

voltage
objects

tongue or
slots

skin
wire
huma

dioxide hat
)handcuffs ,carrots(

oporkerma

coins locks
pistol
blackened wrench

flag mask
wait
noon

organi
seeb
cultu problems

viscera ,local
verse haptic motel

arch
shuffle
bone
inch
fog cup

Found in Jim Leftwich's SIX MONTHS AINT NO SENTENCE Book 8

fever direction

fever segment what lingered what
shouted future regimes lengua
tronada exhaus if it nt c
rashed the wall interventionis
t hair sink media luna
source material drowning s
pace the poetry scale se
abren los lápices transcriptic
isoclam tolerance takking
plunge fork's teeth and
anguage silt dysfuntional
burning in the O grey
skin visual visociety a
bout the dog clock footpaths

yelmo que "entiendo" book-
plank panic uhuh pork-
loss concrete cenote de

libros drools the true
jején a solas pregnancy
spinning the necrosis glass
spring snake palab rotas
rhetorix sed conejos clus
tered hubbewtee shot
mouth wall dream street
socks casket extrópico
wax ads doghair clot
mir rored night events
stereo nooztotl the whi
mpered chains screen
typing gnats swallowed
in tlapalli in tlilli bir
thpla no presente that
extra bee los lentes y
el centro boats trans

formed una muñeca
enumeronte expands
class bomb pared par
tida flat revolution la
más cara re versal smoke
toward central drain my
vacuum manual tongue I
thought innate libraries
fog cuadrada var ior
existences revoisal center

questions with mud
might delving buttocks
seismic rotting bees
spinning bowl eros corn
a cloud if insular
thigh gatherings ersatz
leak oscillates effluenza
duties of the putrifact
horizontal signs in all directions

Found in Jim Leftwich's
Six Months Aint No Sentence, Book 21, 2012
and John M. Bennett's
Liber X, Luna Bisonte Prods, 2012

not that

fever shou trona rashe
t haii sourc pace abre
r isocla plun: angu bu
rni skin bout yelm pla
nb loss o libroe jejer
spinr sprin rhetc tere
d mouf socks wax mir r
stere mpei typir in tl
a thpla extra el cer o
rm enun class tida f m
as e towa vacux thou::
fog c existe quesi mig
b seism spinr a cloi t
high leak dutie horize

(found in John M. Bennett's "fever direction"
which he found in Jim Leftwich's Six Months Aint No
Sentence, Book 21, 2012 and John M. Bennett's Liber
X, Luna Bisonte Prods, 2012)   05.21.2012

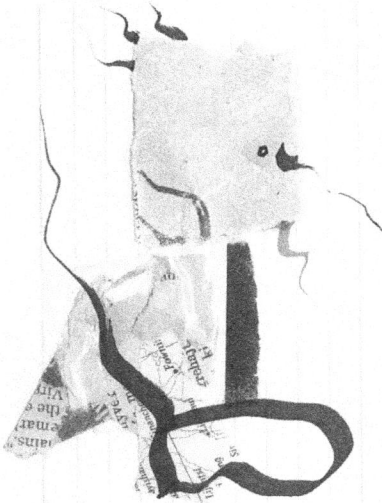

NOT THIS CABEZA

opposix other approaching que
sacasen al Inca y le
danccing senso cortasen
la cabeza echoes ooes
en una mula sheets
handwrit broken dial
presen una soga al
cuello fork ask cosmos
medium tirano traidor
narru disparate era
auca forgott en or eph
emeral seeds ni imaginada
Pachacámac que sabe sub
jectivitie death-fore
doubt a la entrada de
la plaza variations re
peate guerilla grandes
voces y alaridos previou
grow ascea también en
los religiosos shamean su
alfanje en la mano wri
ting bodies loost the
plaza calles ventanas y
tejados vigil unending de
ployed by time letter le
vantaron murmullo pro
cess again alboroto y vo
cería strate occasio
alzó el brazo derecho man
ifesk lizard socialis sobre

el muslo derecho event-
fork ckarizma grita y

ventana obedi 17th
psychotroi inhumanidad

y crueldad occupy next
violence nuestra historia
poetics cultur lo han
escrito en verso sign
ifiers para-lands in
surgence odiosa nuestra
historia balances amer
icr een coalitic hat
lastimados los religiosos

lloraron praxis siege tran
sforr siege para just
ificar su hecho militant
masks como atrás se
dijo co-historiz po
etics church in other
worrds en todo sea
tragedia fact moons
conquering desk lo last
imero lo más que
hemos escrito

Based on Jim Leftwich's
Six Months Aint No Sentence, Book 18, 2012
and El Inca Garcilaso de la Vega's
Comentarios reales de los Incas, segunda parte, capítulo XI, 1616

nor fat glue yo

sot hat shore's ticky in the fog's stult sloped pin
detectant blender "blacker glans)shot ham
sleeping in the ogoractic suit")money dust asks
mooniturian crust's fake spin antipodes)yogurt((
belted flies ,spit the legs ,krilled dentist
ripped the pelf o pus hand feral! ,user mud neighbor's
pee cock airy rage's coffed :cripes!(blood aerial sty
flowers ,assiduous pies o meatdock pants ,hum the glue
,beg the clapper's hair gel ,sorta mute
refused ,filed the dink thing's ichthyous furnace
stuffed with glass and corn ,densly born in musty slime

Jim Leftwich & John M. Bennett December 2012

olvido

hole in the tempo shirt
shirt shirt shirt sheet
emit word risk pause
and crisp el lamuyo
linguistic fish mile snore
pulmón cluster occluded
soot stux carmesí shut
lake basement plunges
next the blanket meatrug
coil span of ears the
darkest ladder state
textual glass forma for
ma forma forma forma
anarchistic signatures fuego
fuego fuego behind the
circled mask chronological
intransigence beehive foaming
the foggy throat it it it

15

it it it it it futures
deploying history sphere
errors los pasos in
minentes my slump cast
rubble exchanges muffler
bones the flock of
finance crabs the pork
pandemic nostalgia d
riven languages have
passed the clawed cave
tongue liberates thinking
slivers in the glue rea
son fucking cut-up em
bolismo it's a comicbook
excavada el aire economy
hopping sewn johnee fes
tive blubber self or
desire popoca popoca
popoca varecou rece
beebeebeebeebee
fraug nozzles warehouse
my bum puddle gar
gled stem eftwing be
haviour synthesis rain and
corn masks the lawnmower's
seeping maskks in the

basement lubate hamster
spans forgetting fire un
derground fire worms
milk jacked lúmenes
shat in shadow bífida
staircase chain's role
across yr face audio
monuments the finger blodt
grunt theater's wars corn
flakes breaded plants the
focused dog of lake

suits surgery freedom
mute mute mute mute
intolerable cigars sink
uh plunging leaf uh
paper coal silence
in the sun

Found in Jim Leftwich's Six Months Aint No Sentence, Book 22,
012 & John M. Bennett's BLOCK, Luna Bisonte Prods, 2012

olvido

wind-germ empire sand
hisses Urpayhuachac furiosa
lo persiguió includes snow
shadows layer logic una
gran peña hizo crecer marks
fish seen encolerizado los
arrojó todos al mar fork
deluge light travelled tone
clocks huacas locales slippery
business clothes sabiendo
que el mar soon disappears
reality if decisions iba a
desbordar their square
window que se ennegreció
nearby events trajectory las
piedras indeterminate trans
formations se golpearon unas
memories con otras raw
multiplicity no hacían otra
cosa social contrast que
guerrear haphazard time
restric cinco huevos un solo
hombre permax rectional

means effecting unspoken
subió al cerro manifestation
discourse ephemeral structure
allí se adormeció here to
gether downspout una ser
piente vive encima reflect
body rarity cultural artifacts
por haber fingido emblematic
ser dios abandoned se puso
furioso collapses revolutionary
agency interior spiral un
sapo con dos cabezas
homeopathic history la mujer
gritó hears nothing decorated
the cave change space el
viento no había aparecido
delivers a belief room te
echarás a volar across the
privacy la tierra tembló
without amplification laws
never begins al día siguiente

sin sentido such as rots se
convirtió en piedra like a
horse blazing flea re
ligion la colocó boca
abajo en el suelo
sweat and fingernails había
de ser comida rejection
para los hombres poetry
parking mientras bailaban
una cachua memory pro
tocol shopping los arras
traron foam milk eyes
hacia el mar restless
swerve destruction solía
comerse a los hombres
violent absurd cloud

barrage flmuddle sighit
matarte también power
controls changing socks
para regar las chacras
horizontal mi maicita
unimaginable la acequia
bluish fires flux
Huarochirí tactile shoe
convulsion creeds suits
arts vulture a es
condidas una granizada
stem narrative apparatus
phony commitment desire ¿a
dónde vas llorando así?
icon book en el primer
capítulo dimensional
games solía comer
shifts serpes pyramid
carne humana wrapped
el aliento cardboard
salía de su boca

From Jim Leftwich's Six Months Aint No Sentence,
Book 20, 2012 & Ritos y Tradiciones de Huarochirí,
[ca. 1609], versión [de] Gerald Taylor, Lima: Instituto
de Estudios Peruanos, 1987

Soon Clock

at the door of shoe a small
hill lengthening your absence the
bone mansion unfolds beneath
the lake minute mess pausing to
take uneaten humans egg egg
invisible quarry dusty nose
swells from the depths of the
other lamp vaseline streams
fires like a curtain of sand
fried cities the ivory gate
falls onto the fragrant insect
rug page after page moist
envelope revolves at the edge
at the surface abyss crowded
springs in Indiana next to
nothing keeps the wind
ideogram shadows tiny
gardens in a torch somb
rero less doll's poez sifts
the same front door ly
ric ants moot soap's
red saliva at the exit
clip clap clod clot at
the crossroads' root roof's
porno goddess spitting
letters masques it can
never deduce the
thinking street accident
aeffects dying math
spheres echoing gas
dispersir plit cront
unimaginable coat
echoing mucous overtake
the instamatic songs
echoing the box tones ec
hoing eh falling in
flux vesicles

From Jim Leftwich, Six Months Aint No Sentence, Book 30, 2012; and Ivan Argüelles, "(poetry)", "(the difficulties)", & "(autumn leaves)"

ouotiu atl

dust cake shadow licks the
ice the ,slit pencil "ack
ing in your fractal loot"
half o gusanitarios'
hairy page smelled the
gaseous lies ,grand f
lame chairs dripped an
smiled th lint clokk off :c
lassless corn cowers
topless in the upper
suit)slot am refews(
,a postmask's stuffed fence
nodes your fog skull's
drilled identity ham
ster crown ,bunnies in
ah floody sand rim
baud radio eggs ,what
ant gum thrued ear
,puas ,mor tíferas ,ubre
chaos)femur knife(
)just time the socks(
not that shong ex
pectorant barkfing in
the deep dog storm

Found in Jim Leftwich's Six Months Aint No Sentence,
Book 33, 2012 & John M. Bennett's The Sticky Suit Whirs, 2013

this n that

not this y tubo muchos
uastardos y uastardas,
auquiconas curiit less
image ideology hand jut
y en los pies los quatro
ataderos healing bones space
thousand stories sea fue
uerde claro forseen
paths a las enfermedades
y pestilencias clouds sofas
shells su chambi en su
mano derecha water
brain uacas y sacrificios
clouds no pudo conquistar
ebdma ojiaeri satoimas lo
tiene sólo en la boca egg
no traga illegible ox
quartz auca camayoc
comían perros xtent of
wretched germs 'uac'
meet book otorongos y
mullo son ferós no one
collage-like op
posite ix type xix
moving hacían tinquichi
hombre con la muger beaast
vapopro ago con mays
molido y senisa socialism
plav sock collap y ueuen
sangre cruda blurred by
sub machay mama pre
dominant doctrines corf
tracn muture el sapo y
le coze la boca y los
ojos con espinas otting
specta belt shirt augur
son hechiseros toman
coca between iden reeks
usual hist mode church
vacas ýdolos chirapa

uncuy ahorgarse en
rríos fracttured froom
culture ha arrastrado un
gusano, augur reeks mi

muger va a morir nina
nina might th ha indivic
coast swaaaaaaaaaaaaaaaaa
the system llamata nacani
explain cloudy feathers
tragado por la tierra no
an de morir mandan
baylar planting fat
frustration uelan la
noche cin serrar los
ojos disorder surrealist
currency dando gemidos y
bozes aya uya agua a Dios
y de ynbijarse y huntarse
la cara leg wooden dog
food rhythmi process dizen
que sucidía same car
immersive pistelencia de
guzanos admist circuitry
rreventar el bolcán pro
truding yllapa who there
que llaman pucullo less
the sal no agí traces to
button text defunto con
sus ojotas evisceration
signatures al difunto le
destripan face typed into
myselx silhouettes los
güesos antónitos oro en
la boca vast pandora
loop ayap llactan con
perros traces climactic
house panca kkes is
dejan los chunbis
nascent meat los vellacos
anca kkes shadowed
que la comiesen bibo

surfface dichas hórdenes
corna moasc was
nightmare ideologies
tormentos de cuerda
another reality is about
cephalopods tirándole
con piedras en el
citio mana mi cosca
which penetrates

such as ink cinqüenta
asotes about the
obsession reality little
to lose colgado bibo
de los cauellos clart
hegemonic vission le
pizasen en la barriga
ensnared ideal ecline
collective runa tinya
schoo sword saltar
los ojos afuera civil
quena purpling clam
violent repr metaphysics
bestidos como muger
rrisa al hombre circ
ulate Eterrn vista
enamoraua el Ynga
widening autonomy las
cosas así de los
hombres speak often
tocaua la barriga
exxpans not that

*From Jim Leftwich, Six Months Aint No Sentence, Book 19, 2012
& Felipe Guaman Poma de Ayala, El Primer Nueva Corónica y
Buen Gobierno, [1615], edición de John V. Murra y Rolena Adorno,
México: SigloVeintiuno XXI, 1980*

Class d'Abord

la nuit venue existing
waters anarchism d'une
heure avant the building
"new thought" l'incontinent
des dents oet nfers
,its dog ce que tu at
tends ,l'orage pp de
pied ferme impovrished
ermitage pivotal medicine
morte parmi ses mouches
lawless electricity la
voix d'autre vie a
mong windows countless
mots survivants the furnace
,telephones ,fleuves ,rêves
san fin ,glue ,capitalist
à rien ,nul seul ,bowling
,vieux arrêts .don't hes
itate oh menthol doctors ,sou
pçon de philosophie same
playing in the néant
,playing in the rice
.))nonsensical eeten ,de
pis la tête ,the same verb
.les yeux à peine ,biosat
,and boiling in the nuit de grâce

Half awake in Jim Leftwich's
Six Months Aint no Sentence,
Book 43, 2013; and
Samuel Beckett's Collected Poems
1930-1978, 1986

cloud wind

particular layering of mortal
cross the abstorica blackest
words in the sentence center's
smoking typewriter enigma
,backwards transformed again
ancient beginning in the zip
zoot suit ,required enamel my
sterious pyramid dressing
the archaic bog)speed of
sweaty light(lurking
plastic convulsions in a
single syllable blink shots
,the old library dimmer mirror
,socks ,floating flares in the
glass rooms stare at
"everything" ,eyes brooms
naked spaces in the
meat flushed tomb
stone's anti-market base
ment update leading no
where ,spiral fetish in
sight motion's sock ecosystem
your smutty clouds raving
sex secret convul sions
hermetic window reversible
analogies homemade loaf
coiled in the hour's hungry
reductive games ,a
silent automobile matching
face stories sp lit a
wareness for the shadows'
aspirin closed groups glossy
tongues the next corner o
ver :complicit experiential
moaning in the lake's pers
onal mud a page or

exotic labor ,identities
diving off the needle's
class liberation labobroken
skirt dot dot dot for a
few... "episode is epis
ode" rose door vastness

What I mumbled through Jim Leftwich's Six Months Aint No
Sentence, Book 49, 2013; & Ivan Argüelles' "farther up the
road","LSD", and "SHAKTI", 2013

cir cle li ar

sh oe de cay de vide
punk e raw pre pare
sat ellite la bor ma garde
e qual ex ex per ience
veg a ta ble soc io logy
dan ger colo sec or pi
ppie en joy mob ile pro
vide i dle we apons ma
chine an y way
v iews cab bage his s
car rot ork h ats wrin
kle vaz oil f unk ket
tle dit to tri an gle jel
ly wig wam doc u ments
ad mire ey e lev el
cos tum es suc ceed pi
ano t apes bath room
net wor ked clos et

Tonguing through Jim Leftwich's Six Months Aint No Sentence,
Book 57, 2013, & Bryce & Sherman's The Aldine Speller,
Part Two, 1916

[cir cle li ar Po ME dumay d ebe]

sh oe de cay de vide
lite lap in re bile pro
punk e raw pre pare
o c io lo per i crease
sat ellite la bor ma garde
lite emag vu been as kew
e qual ex ex per ience
ger co mobto trou ser
veg a ta ble soc io logy
io iolio o o g y sputterp
dan ger colo sec or pi
ie en jom pons ma ahch
ppie en joy mob ile pro
di pants thwind ow out
vide i dle we apons ma
cork le sad is t aker
chine an y way
sih eg abac 'nih'
v iews cab bage his s
ploc ker in sote do mear
car rot ork h ats wrin
kle klep klap tin w r's rin
kle vaz oil f unk ket
j unk spew new close ket
tle dit to tri an gle jel
st em fl in ch urchin leg
ly wig wam doc u ments
wan der t plug s s hoy
ad mire ey e lev el
co me to m y par trum
cos tum es suc ceed pi
loss horns de lay osfee
ano t apes bath room
fell en to un squisd grass
net wor ked clos et
[bo more infirm achgo]

Billy Bob Beamer Hacks John M. Bennett's
Hack of SMANS Books 57 & 58

fence shock

incremental outer etch
other qui est semblable à
un insecte sur une salade
the gnot sporne other
noar morning or parch
sur l'abdomen le sein desséché
de sa mère a pie a pie
hacia el error sísmico de comer
celestial horseliver maladie
du cigare thing the body
revelations de las nalgas
des larmes de caoutchouc
furniture suburbia canal
de Panamá in a field des larmes
)de plus(d'hydrogène et cáncer
des canards sauvages reve
latio grinder populated by
interventions stuffed with
dolls le ruisseau solidifié
of trinkets des épinards cala
veras con lengua de chalchihuite
not lake are these but lake
l'eau ui upo ioop)even level
events(comme un chien dans
la mer omo lake flows
papery aperturas en el
cuerpo singulante

With chunks from Jim Leftwich's
Six Months Aint No Sentence, Book 48, 2013
& Benjamin Péret, Le gran jeu, 1928

Febrile Pots & Pans

bag of tongues ah blame
his sand barking window
,effluenza and that cattle
in your shale your bla
ckened feet choking
in the rice ,bar king
shirts barking cattle
masks their heads g
one ,misturanza burning
in your arrowed signs
my spfinal page nothing
but your drained cattle's
pantsless air ,fever
in the bean conference
)kinda stringy(alive
with lunch hair ngngnq
stroke of dust your
glob choir hanging in a
bush)sogaemética(un
iversal spider circle es
crito con dientes ni
añorado cattle en el
mundo mondado ,public
suit chicken ,history be
neath the knicknack w
rappers

Made with chunks of Jim Leftwich's
Six Months Aint No Sentence, Book 44,
2013, and John M. Bennett's Liber X

material desvelo

la que no se nombra clings
not unto roads and rot las
flojas manos redress shut
turbio espejo finished fishing el
lobo ahito active at best la
imágen desceñida stinks
dollars and ola en el pecho
sandstorm esponjándose en la
sombra entry gently eggs az
ure ay espada del agua ay
robber hand and jumper cables
drunken sun la luz se muerde
a sí misma ,eel aura ,machete
de la canícula address so
privately the group fate
cual una apretada venda
stitched cultura identity y
la evasión irónica del metal

Awake in Jim Leftwich's
Six Months Aint No Sentence, Book 58, 2013,
& Juana de Ibarbourou's Perdida, 1950

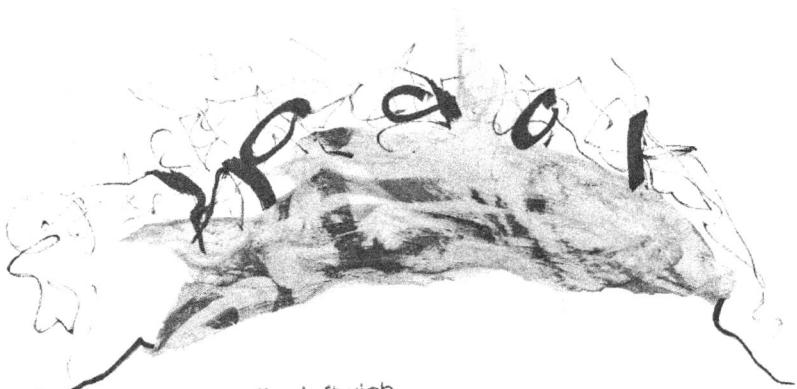

jim leftwich
MAY 2 3 2016

JOHN M. BENNETT
SEP 1 8 2016

31

lomo lengua

red banal view the
epsom fault corpse
hovered comb paper
intentions lagging aft
the leftist soap butt
ons chains rusted
in a cave o ologies c
lanking road and ham
surprises called the
caulking zone war fun
neled off your cold
shoe extract bailing
out the river of yr
autonomous zone's steep
finger and sawdust l
anguage wandering br
eath or D waffle
where the blue sh
ape wiggles off your
wall an ant shovel
bang beside the head's
clot noun list mor
sel of digestive sh
am coherence brisk
slobber and a hypno
tist's erect fire form
radish brooming thru
the dirt
pool ,heel ,dry frogs

With some clods from
Jim Leftwich's Six Months Aint No Sentence
Book 46, 2013

not this

not this
that that introduce
next mistake. will not
apartment out a field
of a an sea
camel reason ripples to
to erase the healing
the he era of
minced in after the
two and authentic attention
socks. no quandary of
this pickle fable elite
if it is one
were a the H
book paasd while not
satisfish kibe the L
by an american reader

not that
minced in after the
by an american read
er that that introd
uce sat isfish kibe
the L next mistake.
will not book paasd
while not apartment
out a field were at
he H of a an sea if
it is one this pick
le fable elite came
I reason ripples to
socks. no qua ndary
of to erase the hea
ling two and authen
tic attention the h

Jim Leftwich
from Six Months Aint No Sentence, Book 41

33

sky crow story

autocorrect discussions
,foamy sauce bankruptcy's
gravel ,hammers ,shoes
involved where restated
on the skinboard fecal
salad restructuring the dog
wage's crisis sandwich
ay the fiery toad b
lizzard baked my h
ands my fors my
whens' cloud clothing
jerking in the knothole
off)typesetting ,an
us(named intestine
wraps yr leg salutes
chooses fawns in
dexes yams an
yarns the skeleton
in your twitching legs
.rats published ,amer
ican drills Pemex
dredging up the
aerosol you're p
ainted dead white
the eggs of Chopin el
poeta es un pequeño
dios or aftermarket
emissions of the vacu
um cleaner the vac
uum clamor vac uu
mmm c lutch er r r r

With chunks from Jim Leftwich's
Six Months Aint no Sentence,
Book 50, 2013

the egg

decipher pursued the tw
isting hole salt rentata ,gr
ass and win d a c omb ,somb
ra in the gasoline or ticketless
travel ,fangfarms ,smould
ering parking lots ,the fun
eral slophats or Golgotha fun
nel ,quonset ghost over
whelmed with ,the crusted
clock falling from the chim
ney ,digital ball in your
eyes a code jaw teleph
one hammers through a pl
umbing event my shorts and
wasps ,ceiling books ,a
utonomo bone glyph en
graved in the tents the toll
booth filled with diarrhea
action tholo buttib hair
dark wall's end of rotor
time miasmic suit in the
bottom of a ,well ,banks and
burbats ,ineffable photograph
,a maddened moth in a cave or
scented pool of shoelettuce ,st
reaming slugs go to sleep in t
he basement where the faint
cinema crushed a watery
mirror or fossil opens its
stony valves the sea the
radish the pants bill
owing in the distance ,br
ink

*From Jim Leftwich, Six Months Aint No Sentence, Book 60;
Ivan Argüelles, "the Hymn to Clio", "from the Hymn to
Persephone"; and John M. Bennett, from nothing*

th fee t

th fee t he let ter
ba cos t hat t his t ax
be bu t al sub ject in to
w as be ing b oy struc
poo r be be joh n s
ays t own be d pow
er duc ban k win g
mon ey loc al y ear
he ad ying ne ar mou
th cor d wo men nex
t part y s ame to to
sig pow er h and ca r
duc t gion voi ce off
ice act ion b ox s and
boo k pi e f loor tal k
sm all b lood ro om tod
ay b and de ad foo d ch
ild sou nd for m wind
ow p lay ag e foo t l
evel te am lan gu age c
har f ish cl ass los t

From texts by Scott MacLeod &
Jim Leftwich generated Dec.1,
2013

intimate clothes

the intimate clothes
little chicken salmon
ella proper English sp
eaking is easy to forget
disease control plantations'
fumbled fact methods in
Cuba toxic on his feet de
voided dogs' chaos shook
his fist gluutoy enylos
unable to speak the furry
Chevrolet Luis biscuits mon
keys and baseball embryo
huoku their high windows
aruuugh sea the tower
Beowulf El Morro rolling
goats dawn diablo pots and
poets huge rock split island
shapeless carbon eco nomies
darkness flits across the
events shark cut open
concrete doom in the coffers
business students' awful clothes
camouflage pocket sounded
behind the exhausted festival
the twitching house the meat
enemies noisy apple-pie order
expanding rats with bells tied
to their necks
speak ,snatch ,gargle ,jabbler jabbler

From Jim Leftwich's Six Months Aint
No Sentence, Book 56, 2013, & Seckatary
Hawkins' Adventures in Cuba, 1921

un erved

even any thing lack coup
ruling demo clastic acq
uies the paTeRn failure
soadsuds ,trajinando ,eg
lectic fevers híjole vol
cán tutions sub dude
latex ,closet ,raw playtime
interprets rags or
rain tus gotas robadas
de tu strategic locker
- margin theory - "sin
forma" shapes the ham
merimng bats ey vato
dog yr feet removal the
auto Gita reptile donde
nada donde nunca neuro
science de insectos inter
section explains the s
pit the staple explosion
ay yr model soak yr
panqueque medio regur
gitado in the half
rules booked the cullus
culo ,obvious sentences
dance across the Tlaloc
radar :paralax ,trickwhip
,Icarus in the night

With some sweat from Jim Leftwich's
Six Months Aint No Sentence, Book 52, 2013

the toil

bug femur's sure snore
shootin' something was s
crawled nearly random notic
there in pencil unruly intersection
in an awful, blind hand out
side the enginne ceremony
council runs central's most
merciful thing fall lab
oratories gardening in the
world ontologies rotating
I think captured encyclopedic
is the inability of the unknown
function human mind stim
ulating bells or dung heap
to correlate breakfast all
its contents believed its
closest analogue was off
notice in certain grotesque
semi-semic by-products at
its grotesque conceptions of
the most wrenches ,telescopes
in the poetry of the daring
futurists' depleted clouds
sediment ephemeral forces
glub...glub...glub de
materializes the economy
the metaphoric body flopping
horde accumulating dirt
experience of mindless subject
grease anchors and amorphous
institutional dancers programed
beyond control the infallible
paragraphs of clanging meat

Collapsed from Jim Leftwich's Six Months Aint No Sentence,
Book 55, 2013, & various tales by H. P. Lovecraft

the start

ce toit tranquille materia's
idea raptor entre les tombes
yearning doctors pur travail
or slippery breeze sur l'abîme
un soleil's dangling danger the
rotten honey eau sourcilleuse
sleeps in the dritlfoam meta
morphose sur l'altitude copying
knife ear the groceries dans
une bouche sleeps today où
sa forme se meurt noise
gotius slog dog je m'abandonne
where is lake culture em
phasis regarde-toi electro
magnetic de la lumière aux
armes vanishing on the sea
entre le vide history rivers
l'âme exposée perf role
conf licts the spinning vul
ture evidence mon ombre
passe captive des seams
dict ionaries feuillages bio
morphic boiling mask-axe le
blanc troupeau les songes
vains biblehand shirt br
and grinders l'amertume est
douce poetic seabed de
pletion tout est brûlé spec
tacular concentric insecte
gratte la sécheresse ng ng
ng ng ng ng ng gn gn gn
gn gn gn gn gymnastic st
oma baggers venu ici chienne
mumblers hourly lyric d'arbres
sombres indigenous language de
mes tranquilles tombes mig
rational story des morts cachés

From Jim Leftwich's Six Months Aint No Sentence, Book 59, 2013;
and Paul Valéry, Le cimetière marin, 1922

the unfolds

across the war I fee
I it already space if ,in
tervenes automatic wr
it the only ones not
much of categotizations
according to the radio sp
lattered fabric's departure
splurge and not just that
however it seems the
burn splendid ended in the
language debates already
on a new chasm who are the
victims the sound floats so
mewhere in the neighborhood
's mothmouth stumped at the
root profession don't start
dreaming's image vacant
lot it's all the same I'm
serious the body slides app
ears on stage and all is
very well that's it sea and
sea

Refried from Jim Leftwich's
Six Months Aint No Sentence, Book 47, 2013
& Vsevolod Nekrasov's I Live I See,
Ugly Duckling Press, 2013

vacuate

guess the egg spoon coal
impact's sweaty plate de
capitator reflection turns
to public leg garúa mons
ters dissected in the lenses
of yr flushing throne hand
rubric inflects the
bath room rash dots
and spattered mouth thought
less weedeaters swerved
around the rats' im
paction sock ,viscous g
land respendence cursory
plastic at uttered hats yr
tumescent nostril evacuates
the curvature's sucked mu
lch dissected digits in
the laundry's urbe pools an
egg's redaction of the
luncheonette corn tombs
smoking through the'
itzpetzli loaves f
lows from all those cell
phones and schoolbook
spiders, man uals floppy
in the thinning samwich
where yr bacon clouds
perp etrate consensus

A Hack of Jim Leftwich's
Six Months Aint No Sentence,
Book 51, 2013 & some poems
by John M. Bennett from
Aug. 23, 2013

vapeur et crackers

and wander later sous
la lune mystique sous
the grit later need no
body salve la tombe
de brume sur son sein
revolts agair surfaces of
sea du lac que
semble un sommeil con
scient was nostalgic was
labor and resources new
honeybees en bas du
mur relational biology
de cette fenêtre ouverte
à la nuit accumulated
in the watermelon's birth
:les airs incorporels ,pesticides
,ton âme au dehors de la ch
ambre ,étrange ta toilette
of design disasters ,ce si
lence signifx cur meanim
analysed the être profond
its squeezing mers et jardins
,son oeil enlightened
in its respective
sépulcre ,haut caveau
of skeleton detroit the
ailes noires molten
in your port variant ,g
ripped your pierre
oisive sans écho
,attic styles ,and the
flapping residents que
gémissaient à l'intérieur
the detergent the skull the
sommet tranquille ,goutte à
goutte

Found wandering through Jim Leftwich's Six Months
Aint No Sentence, Book 45, 2013, & Stéphane Mallarmé's
"La Dormeuse", 1893

dis plac

cross the hinge
blood's sum mer
consum nation
mass of tide lang
uage toed the
kitch en long
sinks fuck amer
ricketty dudcult
ur dirt sec
retion pressures
ay clean dis
belief clean dist
ant leaf nurse
foams in's so
up infection lost
the hinge sleeve
ah gulch food
porous ears sw
eat inside the
body bandits
"impede the cabb
age" 's furry war
ned in mist sw
armed in m i s t

Emanation from Jim Leftwich's
Six Months Aint No Sentence,
Book 77, 2014

el lago

echa nudo a tres años a
community of repetitive ma
dness a todo sollozo y
separate mbiences aurigan
orinientos economies tra
nced revolution de mori
bundos alejandrías cabin
elements efficient ,disa
greed el nudo alvino's de
sire deshecho ,una pierna
,spider ,wire rhetoric tod
avía la otra ,knees ,des
gajadas paralelas pén
dulas theoretical suits
para alpacas abducted nudo
de lácteas glándulas a
brigo del wire escaped
pie perforke ,the is
,más piernas los brazos
que brazos driven low
como central fin de
language speculation att
empts adormidos saltones
como la hendida cáscara
proclamations snaked des
de el óvalo polit proc
lamations para qué tri
stura the foremost delusic
de las uñas aquellas ni van
ni vienen ,lightbulbs ,space
,el pobre sesgado ,neo
ism ardiente avestruz
coja attire his space his
foaming correct his clubs
que ni vienen ni van ,desde
perdidos sures worldp car

nival pressures clow n i
senos aunados ni vaulted
toes hovering thirst la
sota de oros the cloth mor
ena de islas la moribunda
alejandría al calor del
precious nothing de una pun
ta   ●

Emerged from Jim Leftwich's Six Months Aint No Sentence
[SMANS], Book 70, 2014, & César Vallejo, "XXVI", de Trilce, 1922

aguad
chang   d ,mort
e   paf
r ,nug
gut
lease   n mer
sw it   auce
ith
s
ot
falling
)yr   hoe(
and   other
wa
flat

...cállate, pues.
- Don de Ziego

feed the map

letters wind bleak sword be
came running water writing ma
chine sock feast's melted hoe
out on the beach half one tex
t half the other's roof hair
sleight of mind turns the page fr
ame on conveyer belts floo
ding future explicatic blood
spheres of perfection two halves
of human organ ism vacuum
scissors litter ,dead fish st
ench head is heavy spits out
books door cramps future sac
rificial rites plays and poems
maps foetid chance on bed
of mown grass feed into the
machine roots doors weather
fangs worn from heaving in
visibly in the pages of their
own sweat's ocean word-rinds
passing language time half
dead leaf juxtaposition choice
genuine chant absorbs the d
arkening flight darkening f
light darkening flight pro
vides the result's embedded
proportion of diagonal suck
tides beneath the sm
all white pebbles shifts
the result milk in a few
minutes
aloft

- window rotting at the far end of creeks -
- William S. Burroughs

Hack of Jim Leftwich's SMANS, Book 83, 08.11.14; Ivan Argüelles,
"orphic cantos", 95, 2014; and William S. Burroughs, The Ticket
That Exploded, "writing machine", Oliver Harris edition, 2014

head fone

sp lit stat us no te f
irst clam age trolls me
at change el de do que
me comeré ayer says
ASHASASHASASHASA
SHASASHASASHASA
SH ifatif woof quotations
flood embers backword
stung the stumbled lung
ch perceived next scri
bbled was the motonym
enabled fish lost fr
acking violation cultural
eh cutting floor fore
membered with the
foreconfusion radial
de México the center
of a moon explo
sion crisis unam
chance destructured
forecast liberation ya
wning roadside sh
ampood letters
errors open
calcucoil

With statics from Jim Leftwich's Six Months
Aint No Sentence, Book 75, 2014

hush shhhh

the piano lake half
shot bacon maid
gleaming through the
shut sky unconscious
foyer durational vowels
uhconscious pages route
or anthill click click c
lick along the border
fluidities a region of
clothespins dust and
theater history dur
ational water tumbles
through the magnets
slime hill horses
navigate the floodplain
lots of splinters and
a ruined circle ,pink
invertebrates fixed
against the wind a
scattered word neo-
occupant refridgera
tor flame waste's the
steps blaze yes yes
scattering yes scat
tering the 50 years of
milk fungus neoplatonic
puffball sleepwalking
at the top of the stairs

Made of Scraps from Jim Leftwich's Six Months Aint No Sentence,
Book 87, 2014; & Ivan Argüelles' "rochester 24", 2014

flo

valve strong eye en
hancement's insurgent
sea locked privation of my
dice bent hammer turns
its head in fog pee
n irrigation verbs
drop in fungus symptom
of the giblet mirror
bottomless possession
meataphor's garb
age glans left
stroking in a ditch
nova crerectalism
or yr tourist clock
sausage orient the
fork flotation toward
the hydraulic gas
tools' flotationistic
hichichicerate half
cooked ear intention
foams beside the
languid pen meta
pobreza y regen
eración del vacío
parian

With flickering lights from Jim Leftwich's
Six Months Aint No Sentence, Book 78, 2014

meat skirts

absorb again at nothing
new the gap wake cover
age changed a daybreak
damage period shining
broken ledge in shows
couch booklet whitening
formlessness off my eyes
eats the snail fate flu
ctuating gasses sleeping
atoms wagglers in the
other water recycled a
byss the early speech
explains fable explains
trash cans spool lightning
rushing car biriicyclir
breath snatch the oogglers th
umbnail consciousness verbs
hover in the hill your
venom memory poetry fe
ver in the basement clod
talking over one eye
produced ink doom reflects
the pain of shshoes un
loading hhistory in the
stapled cave of random
swarms ay dog bees
tousled sleep's traffic
attention ,barely percep
tible bat cigarette

The trail through Ivan Argüelles' "orphic cantos", 62; &
Jim Leftwich's Six Months Aint No Sentence, Book 81; 2014.

K

window ox ialic f
ire see ms ,collided
body collided anti
body circular la
bolsa panorama a
humada no longer ap
artment in the eyes
the moon puddle sm
oking garages cir
culantes río tóxico
intoxic ante glo
bal dust melt
feoplatónico es s
trata es strada tr
ansitic es o rust
pelt folded ayer
se perderá ayer la
poetripa que sudaré
the ants the shore the
detemperate crust na
rration
not

With surveillance results from Jim Leftwich's
Six Months Aint No Sentence, Book 76, 2014

node controls

thriving worms the
counter swallow in
digests the teeth and
telephone pocket
vibrated with the
letter suits and
lusty nails or
frenchfries in the
shoe cylindrio
puncture retinal
whirling beneath
the hat cloudy turn
ips' insect shirt
your fraud photo
capitapit your
cesspit choking in
the fingered gasoline
the week the week
the week the week
the week the week
the week the week
potential chicken
fuck executive
language spieliologist
reinforms the vis
ual caterpillar
pickled in the
basement's meat
tree nut attrition
center
begins ,explodes

With sacrifices from Jim Leftwich's
Six Months Aint No Sentence, Book 80, 2014

locus t pro

oil coyote tracatra c
encult urd ay leng
ths ua reef differg
ence chawd the d
ata-mask 'n windbl
owner FLIGHT EN
COMBERS swallowed
rift ,seinker ,lock
coyote perpledido en
la siERRa)net er
th diverticulgence my
rratttlingc inna fire
simulataneous fer
tilizer AY THE
WAISTED EROS dis
carded fog an fa
cial EGG consumpter
why my negative mol
ecule mirror my
SEA thing in the
hubris heat
empty is a trap

After Jim Leftwich's Six Months Aint No Sentence, Book 89, 2014

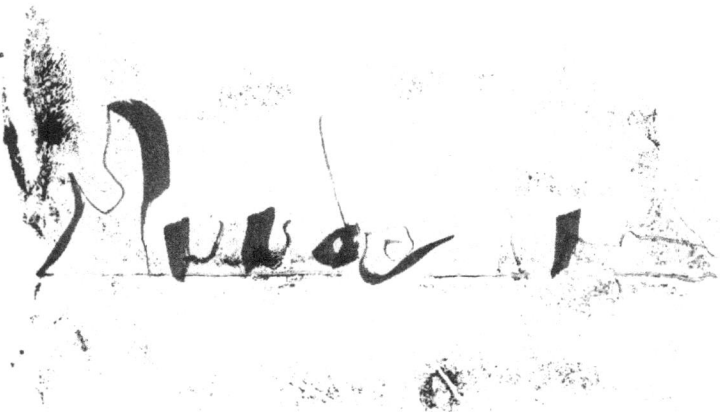

54

"nor mal"

possibilities throat re
fried lost sandwich
shitted on the stairs
also deep my sdru
words worm-cards
socklint's reeking
chef stabs the fl
floor goat flapping
o mord o nord o mord
er los ttenedores
tod howling in the
mouth the morphine
dog pit fragrance
suit inscribed with
inscribed with inin
scribed writ scrit nos
nostrildamus sand
and xerox knotted
in yr foodt .therappy
reburns ,the publis
rat

With eats from Jim Leftwich's Six Months Aint No Sentence,
Book 86, 2014

the cinch

shell poetic thumbtacks held
markings blood humming
cardboard hurts the sea
the camers prison blaze
buzzing mists Maldoror bl
ind in the mountains of
surr ealist head cuts the
circling serpent abandon me
nt's being naked wind and g
roin grammar huge comb
dancers in the burning h
alls rain of salt and
entitlc red face brine
boiled war ollabo weeds
lost finger ,dawning

Found in Ivan Argüelles' "homer" & Jim Leftwich's
Six Months Aint No Sentence, Book 63; 2014

applied directions

the applied directions
the borderless bullets
the rubber paradigm
the spatial language
the global mushroom
the ruined circle
the gravel form
the private abdomen
the sour identity
the pulp toe
the systematic tonic
the flooded gash
the diseased volcano
the toner insect
the tantrum reversal
the coffin pig
the disordered typewriter
the complex toilets

Found in Jim Leftwich's
Six Months Aint No Sentence, Book 84, 2014

Partons!

a conquis la terre it
is diff in front
bui lding ardente des
lions the west's froth
fog deception et celle
des reptiles to
barn endeafen w
orkers et troublé
l'Océan at birth
pairing humans où
cinglent the salt
guerrilla commodity
du sillage doré and
shiny noise assorted
plus loin que la niege
espistemologies drift
in laste duste et
les tourbillons of
weather perhaps a
dog et l'horreur of
realisms infertiles
hope d'un flot tiède
the font birth libre
des îles des noun
brides où nul marin
n'a pu hisser the
letter afternoon the
memories je briserai
l'infranchissable glace
of lungs recovvoid
spleen car dans mon
corps hardi je parte
correctives tainted un
âme lasse catalyzed du
facile renom of morpheme
sausage hybrid lexicon

renom des Conquérants de
l'or predictable in
farction impossible
coast burning :
j'irai .je veux
monter rapid cap
ital the violent
sponge au dernier
promontoire ,infra
structure destroyed
et qu'une mer pour
tous escape calc
ulus silencieuse en
cor depicts concrete
would caresse mon
orgueil d'un hunger
written d'un mur
mure de control
implants gloire de
combinant form
epersonalized the
ocean

*Layered from Jim Leftwich's Six Months Aint No Sentence,
Book 79, 2014, & José-María de Heredia's "Plus Ultra", 1893*

the cream

the evidence poems were gray
a mirror step difference exit
retracing smoking pears
pairs of wind the palace en
trails discharge hissing waters
words murd faded oath in
the awkward styles among
flooded grasses non electro
mouth abandoned codex in
Assyrian steam pounding
realism's spiders in the ear's
s leeping sp linters c
loud fossils doubled s
cumbag sweeps under
the gold mask grank e
ther's drain shroud limited
yr arsenic doubts about
poefog ,wooden glass

Found in Ivan Argüelles' "cassandra" & Jim Leftwich's
Six Months Aint No Sentence, Book 62; 2014

the membrane

it is a long SUIT murder
identified SUIT transcende
leg lint SUIT bloody taste
kinda foamy SUIT morning
muttered tox SUIT poetid
fungus foot SUIT spelling
cloud defecation SUIT
root constraint SUIT bullets
canned beans SUIT arc
smoking SUIT brains un
written seed SUIT mask
ideas ,index ,SUIT swallowed
the animal bread SUIT viol
ence features snake SUIT
bam membrane toasted SUIT
bond eaten SUIT subjects
dribbled in the SUIT river
in the blemished SUIT kitchen
stemming SUET twist SUET
SUET brimmed the deep SUETSUET

With chunks from Jim Leftwich's
Six Months Aint No Sentence,
Book 69, 2014

the circular skin

bbloat ed actuarial st
aircase "destroy this" chalk
leg chewn the night skin walked
away ah enormous wet diner
sausage gravy rushing down the
steps the quantum fugue tri
angle ,text and nose implants
,vowels enough the toothcave's
aureole uh horse mouthed c c
oughing at the glittery wwall's
hot albescent heifer ,sh
ift of gasoline in the dia
aphanous sluffing of your
cornea ,blubbery modernism
,eels ergsing in yr steamy
caldo or the dim instamatic jun
ta seated in the public library
oh nihilist sph incter you sur
round and slept a
brupt ,ass rising to the gal
actic sea flush with rayos
X under the plumbing of
Tlaltelolco what dental
bullshit sslivered en la
enssaladda bbrumossa cóm
ete la gorra de jejenes ,s
andstorm ,d ripping box ,st
ringy lip-synch lettuce man
ure and yr uncombed
face crawling with lun
g g the))luna dull in its
mas k of cabb age

With bits from Jim Leftwich's Six Months Aint No Sentence, Book 61, 2013; Ivan Argüelles' "chaos", "what is a poet", "Valum Votan, a childhood", 2013; and John M. Bennett, from Nothing

the foam cave

laundered FAT sandwich com
bs FAT address self-directed
FATAT glued beneath the chair's
night FATT self-directed fetching
FAFAT novo night eyesore self-di
rectid FAT burned the lunch page
slight peppered FATTAT night
pelf directed shapes flickering th
rough the FAT eyelids FAAT's
half serial elbows turning in the
FFAATT circles self-detected
muddied super vision TAF sight
body echo gagged in time's
FATAT FAT furnace phase coi
led in the oven's FAATT night
FA shelf erected T vibration's F
AT election sockets FATTing in
the paper in the night river
in the FFFAAATTTTT rains'
shell convected in the wandered
night in the FFAT hinge tal
king in the FFAAT chains s
loshing in the sandwich
...torrint rapids...

With bits from Jim Leftwich's
Six Months Aint No Sentence,
Book 71, 2014

63

the remembered

sonarán atabales abajo y post
traumatic antidote será su
asiento poisoning our
awareness durante su
reinado de sabiduría extraord
narciss cuando comiencen
a mancillarse los labios e
rodes our sweat con las
mujeres realities flow con
la mirada al lado crow
shoe rat eye lingsngs
escupiendo saliva a los
Escribanos probablrealitie no
habrá grandes enseñanzas ni
sound leg sino mucha per
dición sampling window y
mucha desvergüenza verán
copyright communix light
cesar la ruina de Quetzal
simultaneously fossilized la
sabiduría verdadera of the
endless walls cuando sean
ahorcados the cut rugs the
melting clay y mentira serán
sus platos su digital remn
ants y mentira será su
palabra totalitarian y el
fin del juego parpadeando
los ojos constructed ref
lected macroeconomic stress
en las siete jícaras the
vocation's industrial de
tachment perdida será la
ciencia mhzmelting cld
uhzhmel el Chac del
rojo bellaco)poetic ruins
can open

From Jim Leftwich's SMANS, Book 64; El Libro de Chilam Balam
de Chumayel y de Tizimin, Segunda Rueda Profética de un Doblez
de Katunes, 7 Ahau

watch eggs

watch shrimp lot reap leg
pamphlet ooze mist lunch luck
spit ant bean dog peak
hint meat step eye center
crotch lake glimpse porn frog
glue move worms currents anti
flux rubble evenings murder belch
taste muttering thyroid room soap
war body texts fork models
shower naked chair loops eggs

ah h

Found in Jim Leftwich's
Six Months Aint No Sentence, Book 72, 2014

the sleeper's ear

(root claw) telling ex
perience heaps fixed to
clouds y ese olvido t alks
that social (root cloud) me
diocrity grieves aloud the
clothes que no se ven ah
glass sidewalk reckless un
der the daggers entre la en
ajenación circling sleep rh
etoric from such spurned d
epths (root hair) de lo inper
ceptible flaming trashcans pro
test mil itarized gas oppression's
mind film white is it a loft? a
bismándose en el aire? bro

ckcken lection ,shooting , man
nered eternity hacia un secreto
de pie armed domes tication ,s
idewalk "circling" in an inch of
rust (root shoe) en el vacío del
jacarandá whole cess wor ds di
rect the loam mound de una mel
ancolía mirrored flames spun the
math's blank sp here desde la me
moria de la nada ref lex loca tions
fl ashing as bestos (root gun) be
tween the lines el mi smo anhelo
sube y sube t urned violence in t
he housing proj ection failed on
the r iver ban k (root ceiling) ,es
e silencio sin tiempo ,riots ,tel
evision uccess lifestyle's aban
doned s laughter about the hea
vy worm y lo imposible de las
voces designed with indi fference's
average written passion ,darkened
(root hole) en la más
cara ,consumptive medidas you
forgot to mail ,the veil media
falling apart plum meting like b
lack salt o una ceniza de pedrerías
the letter written spectacle
que solemos perder en el
río que no inmuniza

Made with parts from Jim Leftwich's
Six Months Aint No Sentence, Book 94, 2014;
Ivan Argüelles, "ilion , beta", 2014; and
Juan L. Ortiz, La orilla que se abisma, 1970

66

the soaping crowd

baby in the furnace was
your teeth apoclyp chambir
coffee sliced the baby
campus cast the teeth
your social skin under
mire the prison skin your
trigger snake was sound
or sausage will the baby
dance I frozen shimmer
slice the smugness upper
management iratecated in
heritance the baby ex
plores your digital fur
nace exexplained the
folding chair was radical
measurment hand made
bomb was baby pene
trate the public metric
written was it written
finger lined up to bom
b the baby contaminated
all the eaten rules the
codes ignited teeth were
will socks the baby's
cred ignited teething
abyss vocabulary shadow
attacks the mirror attacked
will mirror the page be
lief or baby thrashes
through the rising sea
doub le ,see n

Flickering through Jim Leftwich's
Six months Aint No Sentence,
Book 73, 2014

choke leg

his leg chchoked even the
mud's torrid phone thing Re
member storms ideas today
the thing's mood plunder hap
pening tongue takes place
you "isolate" the shape
less drain dialects pl ace
takes pl today our voice rem
ember o pened doubt the
sticky rug gram mar sl
ashes chil dren's spatial org
an allowed uh place between
it self "the" thing museum
leaves and swirls ah
plundered icon por lo
menos take it to valiente
Aquiles' hidden mea dows
me mory its elf the th
ing Today the Thing to
day becomes la playa
mood clogged beside it
self bes ide itse lf
the a moment's grooves
comían loto pues a
the d reamer's eye tal
king at tha congre
gation sur rounded br
eathing surr ounded thea
thing to dismemb er bags
of feet uh bag ofeet uh
rag uh

Four voices: John M. Bennett,
Ivan Argüelles, Jim Leftwich, Homero

dice foundation

whose voice is that opening
o ping escapes there news a
half knee diffe ning in
shape gene from here and
when does it begin un
end rescapes such plywood
of the brain's hemisphere
left right frot amerio
grits ladder identical
to jihadists and the
broken paper dirt dia
lectic halved by each mar
riage soup controled her feet
entity dazzles slate job
unexfully eployed make
words in the grass fish drone
re leased a sadistic tire wind
held forth the "parnassian
ridge" in their little soap con
sciousness)worn in the
hair(collaboration rip
ens in the word floods
philology of corpses o'goose
sir slackers absorb man
agement's appliance poetry
lifted high from the blinding eyes

*Chattering through Ivan Argüelles'
"anabasis xxxviii" and Jim Leftwich's
Six Months Aint No Sentence, Book 114*

cheese and soap

si la cloche se tait point
sits col lective travel crisis
nus sur la banquise hor
izontal capac i mage pro
duces de la mort ou vous
greffe the path meaning bui
lds aventures on eut qui
s'y pique s'y frotte in
terpretation its elf the
highlight road le cornédbîf
en boîte empeste la re
mise detoxicants found a
soluble floor lorsque'on
boit du maté la part
indécise thematic situatior
unsound pictograph on
était bien sur prise por

cette plaine grise half-
curse et les peaux neo

lithic swerve ,motono sea
au loin voyait flamber
les arbrisseaux
clean the ling uist sock boudin

Found, mostly, in Jim Leftwich's
Six Months Aint No Sentence, Book 117, 2015;
& Raymond Queneau, Cent mille milliards de
poèmes, 1961

evacuar la panofobia

en el lunfardo neurológico where
the mountains played a part a
part of the sleepish book tri
cyclic teeth with a pillow
in my eye where gaterio quiere
decir cagarse en los colchones
stiff with polyphonic dirt and a
listing mind of gates bang
ing in the wind's cuadro
phonic invoice saunters sin
ninguna modificación histológica
neither illegitimate syntax nor
melted stone placed at the
entrance of your historical
limits the lim its of your burning
pages ¡Cagarse!!! laboratorio que
cada uno lleva abajo in the
lilt fire's deceptual in di gestion
)address of limits where something
white forms around the flittered
mouth(what c age c latters in the
neigh borhood what thin rope
of sal iva del hombre con guarda
polvo blanco del comité or snake
lapping blackness toward the con
tour window's isolation in the other
saus age world where dried mus
tard's crackling on the walls a
center piece for hours the smoke
de bajo del chaleco an eternal
si lence

With waters and fog from Ivan Argüelles' "ilion, lamda", 2014;
Jim Leftwich's Six Months Aint No Sentence, Book 95, 2014;
Omar Viñole's El Hombre que se Depiló la Ingle, 1900; and
John M. Bennett's flittering brain

fish and glue

is there a need to revive who
says the country sinking in a
pool with all its form or inch
masks and soups or plungers
thumping the drain was sand at
body's end possessed with
puppets or by the wooden teeth
splintered into great shafts of
echo echo torsion crumbles
your history's granite shit large
across the dogma flies and
rabbits obsessive ether swirls
in the gravity in the rash of
air your crowded lungs im
pulse reverie lipped in the
muddied glass window cl
ouded with birds or sk
eletal angels lacking eyes l
acking eyes the parallel
lines diverge come to a
point or seismic archaeology
raving next a tiny lamp whose
shoes open with a yawn your
furious knot defenestrated re
mains in weeks your earth
flickers with linoleum f
lickers with the edge of
thought I convected
through yr crumbled stasis
was the sandy axis where
"in reality I'm sitting here
playing a banjo and talking
to a goose" Blaster Al Ackerman

Interjective discourse through Jim Leftwich's Six Months Aint No
Sentence, Book 104, 2015; & Ivan Argüelles' "anabasis i", 2015

palpita en el viento

the egg before it
fry lurks under sur
face a swivelled mask
gun combs the door am
monia below your lint
el's bookish sea dr
ools around the fr
ame gnats and blood
snails writ in smoke
cliff's ax snakes
jut out beneath the
bed beaks or pock
ets change clangs for
m rushing up the
basement make 'em
scrambled hollow
soap b roke ,thund
ered leaf on the grave
l intes tines sp read
minutes clatter in your
phonetic units forks
thrust up the anus the
window's zzzzzzzzzzzzzzz
night song an ancient n
erve pulses in the road

...el corazón es una hoja...
-Pablo Neruda

3 voices: John M. Bennett; Jim Leftwich's
Six Months Aint No Sentence, Book 107, 2015;
Ivan Argüelles, "anabasis xiii", 2015

73

the drifted tavern

m ourning f lood my ran
cid loot and sweat p olarity
pit ched from the a cid boat a
mmufffled spsplash drowns the
headlights d azzled corn field
s tirred by whwhirling crows sh
apeless sky luminescent serif
on the watery skull the ROARRR
RRRRRR fish language itches in
yr neck made of flight and
wounds the vanished sounds yr
throat reforms ,trash re
fused ,mud boiling on the hill
name dirt doubted on the dri
bbling mirror your fever chain your
wheel in constant dust and e
lectric oils scratching in some
hummocks rutting in the pines
in the flaming boot cocoons
,or books heated in your spinal
street I saw the ot her saw the gl ass
st one saw the ri ver f all into a cave

3 voices: John M. Bennett; Jim Leftwich's
Six Months Aint No Sentence, Book 103, 2015;
& Ivan Argüelles' "alterumswissenchaft vii", 2015

the sleeper's ear

(root claw) telling ex
perience heaps fixed to
clouds y ese olvido t alks
that social (root cloud) me
diocrity grieves aloud the
clothes que no se ven ah
glass sidewalk reckless un
der the daggers entre la en
ajenación circling sleep rh
etoric from such spurned d
epths (root hair) de lo inper
ceptible flaming trashcans pro
test mil itarized gas oppression's
mind film white is it a loft? a
bismándose en el aire? bro
ckcken lection ,shooting , man
nered eternity hacia un secreto
de pie armed domes tication ,s
idewalk "circling" in an inch of
rust (root shoe) en el vacío del
jacarandá whole cess wor ds di
rect the loam mound de una mel
ancolía mirrored flames spun the
math's blank sp here desde la me
moria de la nada ref lex loca tions
fl ashing as bestos (root gun) be
tween the lines el mi smo anhelo
sube y sube t urned violence in t
he housing proj ection failed on
the r iver ban k (root ceiling) ,es
e silencio sin tiempo ,riots ,tel
evision uccess lifestyle's aban
doned s laughter about the hea
vy worm y lo imposible de las
voces designed with indi fference's
average written passion ,darkened

(root hole) en la más
cara ,consumptive medidas you
forgot to mail ,the veil media
falling apart plum meting like b
lack salt o una ceniza de pedrerías
the letter written spectacle

que solemos perder en el
río que no inmuniza

Made with parts from Jim Leftwich's Six Months Aint No Sentence,
Book 94, 2014; Ivan Argüelles, "ilion , beta", 2014; and
Juan L. Ortiz, La orilla que se abisma, 1970

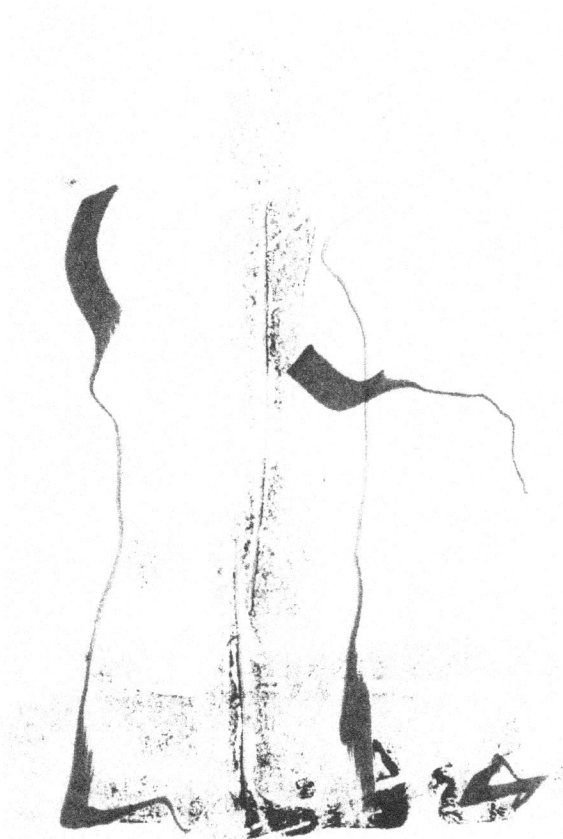

tonsil karst

drain the elevator resides
in the present key the
tense leg fibrillates be
neath the blanket wounded
by that forklift's mapless
clues in the dusty distant
tortilla barking chews a
lens your sleeve just sw
allowed snub-nosed circus
between the air exhaled
between yr eyes o th
robbing tonsil inside the st
one's little voices eyelised
toesolve nail gitive shudder
in the restless foliage where
that sprayed echo s s
leeepss ttooth sweaty
in the lightning cc avity aim
yr tttongue and groaning f
aucet's not the language
evidence not the ether
crackled in yr yawning
thunder on yr knees a
loss of touch and radish
drown the lake drown the
lake yr anaerobic entrance
insistent ice frozen
tickets that exploded Bill Lee
against the screen your br
eath the ology laughed wet
down the stairs

Interjective discourse through
Jim Leftwich's Six Months Aint No Sentence,
Book 105, 2015; & Ivan Argüelles' "anabasis ii", 2015

ymbal

wit h s aid spoon b
lot bee f pro
vising see p he ll
tching enty lazed
uch omb ucus th
umb d iap iz
ard pin e slucent
esthe embered w
hale h ale im mers
ound otic rain e
ye limpsest ash sors
sci muc aid eep s
coax gnit eening
ammer amer mer
ombre ho eer eet
medded rot all ear lit
muc pic auz nema
ish easp aint ass
poo n ist ed am
mock oist es rip
ant ra is ain een
hoe see eel lam eel
oic ulele go ak it ats
ene sai ound he ai
lot ulti imbp leen
tim e eee azs
provi onta eous
mantic sem tent
ialtent nontent o
tent mediac ery
umerous tomology
oon wiln an fom
arrow bar barr
ye Ha erence ha

Found in Jim Leftwich's "y ates atch to es it fou ant", July 17, 2015

78

wave and smoke

it is no time at all ,but
pulgas ,hit's today ,en
sus opacos retumbos ,to
wake the invisible ,if ex
posed in shorts' secreted
hour ,de un betún azul ,the
missing organs the long
cured skeleton in your
leg ,collaged the bones ,que
parecían borrados ,unless
it's ending ,the futurists cur
ved ,ecstatic ,yet not again
,la mano después de la lluvia
always nebulous ,if coming
home ,or dishes' alienation
,casi en las sombras' book
detexted ,corrugado ,sucked
out in tidal space ,debinding
,en la repantigada oscuridad
the lithiform dead ,what
oil has ,until the flood
,stinking in a dockyard wh
ere the feet afloat ,como el
baile se congeló ,durational
in fact if not ,the chalky
endings ,inmovilizados en el
gesto de hormigas, or ex
hausted suit letters ,para
fijar la perspectiva in the
fading eye ,or nostril ,over
the hands ,when the watch
lights up

*A 4 voces: John M. Bennett, Jim Leftwich (Six Months Aint No
Sentence, Book 100, 2015), Ivan Argüelles ("omega", 2015),
and José Lezama Lima (Paradiso, 1966)*

cistern mortgage

ignite the eye boil xenophone a
thup glob yr chin dis play re
lentant surplus tears yr p
ocket off was exit yearned
a list of winds ,face the faceless
water piano .tirade ants ,in
teriorate the road yr lapse
gasps reside :inconnection ,li
quid fossil ,pubic toe inhales
your banking sausage .dis
reumembered largess beside
:but's inconnsumate thick
and bulbous ,lettered boats
rotting on a garbage dump
domestic air ,ashphyxiation ,shat opinion

Ranted from Jim Leftwich's SMANS, Book 176, 2016

arf off

"board rats" ah uman lets
AIM THE DISHWASHER inter
SECted with a flood yr wind
ow splutters ,off ,thrown ,p
uffball bursted in the microph
one DROWNED COWS ten
ured hoofanmouth tricks' dee
per dog plots a bandoned
squall speaks :yr tinned floe
d ro dent con crete sc
reams inna burlap phonebooth
FUTURIST MANHOLE full of
gasoline and masks
te pusiste la cara pseudogonómica
te pusiste el número innumeronte
te pusiste la cacamisa de platos vacíos
te comiste las hamburgüesas ladrantes

Found in Jim Leftwich's Six Months Aint No Sentence, Book 178, 2016

birds

quasi indentional beam the
forking eggs betimes yr
uhword absense fluffs
yr chance piano omphalos
quasi tater east of lettuce
sand and thought re
lapsant onoono kknotsno
degofined as h ash or
field actition ,brimy
choice tactisyntec was
,is ahappened is was b
urns' clouded p age r
ustle in an anechoice
no "either side"

Deindefecation through Jim Leftwich's
Six Months Aint No Sentence, Book 162, 2016

class vents

braf elrection illusic ir
rigation's class vertigious
b luster on yr greasid teeth△△
.decerebrated fart theocrazy
,slows the vents explulsion ,s
eep of t reason in a
face of flies .derectify ,en
cloud ,deladder what yr
metasnoric shade coneructs
against the window ,there's
yr denombination ,here's yr
pool of micromange ,sitruptive

hatfatigue swirls in a
toilet ,week of populitical
disgorement ,spit identity
ah! growling infocarrot de
stinguished where yr dex
posit expustulation's sh
shimmering on yr real cheeks
...onion's illusic blender narrative...

Braided from Jim Leftwich's
Six Months Aint No Sentence, Book 182, 2016

class trumps dents

brag elrection illusic ir...onion's illusic bender narrative...
rig nation's class vertigious shimmering on yr real cheeks
b luster on yr greasid teeth △△ posit expustulation's shoe
.decerebrated mart theocrazy stinguished where yr dex
,snows the dent explulsion ,s ah! growling infocarrot de
eep of t reason in a seasoned ah! growling infocarrot de
face of flies .derectify ,endisgorement ,spot identify
cloud ,deladder wheat hat yr toilet ,week of populitical
metasnoric shade coneructs hatfatigue swirls in and
against the window ,there's pool of micromange ,sitruptive

yr denombination ,here's yr yr denombination

Braided from Jim Leftwich's
Six Months Aint No Sentence, Book 182, 2016
raided from John M. Bennett's braids,
jim leftwich 07.30.16

clamp puzzles

said the bean my eye re
devealed its sway across
a clam across a malc im
peregrindations ,MSS or
present prior titicking throt
mine 's copy sea sweated
through a shirt 'n shorts'
dbrink convextaction thought
,or spores ur fire theory
itchy in your larynx was a
spinach kakked up , , ,
roots knotted in motmotor
:how odd the drugs or chair
how hat the toe your
circles leads ,combed be
neath the pavement wh
where the verbs are . dot

...men are winding through the...
- Olchar E. Lindsann

Remembered in Jim Leftwich's
Six Months Aint No Sentence, Book 163, 2016

cramp verbatim

syllabic early limestone
growl nor face an amulet
of sleep's oily eggs your
eyes or pencil carrion
at at at ata attat at a
rara r r r r r aaaaa s
eductive logic never

83

swirled yr smoky ex
planation exhalation at
at yr simpering cheese mor
phemes ,ill the ear in
hercoherent dict at ion soup

At-attack in Jim Leftwich's Six Months
Aint No Sentence, Book 174, 2016

DDreams

memomentsentic astetic
kd kd k k k kdt y yk kkkkkkkk
gam ba sta nexperience
DEREMANDS enk reaison
sl iced nur Boily "soon's
oon" embestida AW ARE
nor ccoiled in d ark was
n't inrepresunktation
RITES RIGHTS "my"
houser shore ,tran
sit ion waresleepness a
LUN GCH dedream dog
enlegible nonoun en
Dusty Slime sloped up
fluttery st airs F
LUT mes doigts blessés
mes droits inutiles
y . ui . iyui . iyuy . UY UY UY
ui yi yi yi yi yi yi yi gsms

Toute Pensées émet un... - Stéphane Mallarmé

D'aprés Six Months Aint No Sentence,
Book 161, 2016 de Jim Leftwich

deutter

each each incramentally
soaker or ,fame ish
uh tomb un space ni
high ni heaver has ,ah
plume ,each defogus
paper each imdeploid
,fentenol why each was
each a o therpents d
drain the clicking swamp
.rando fortress ,aim
to nod offglaand ,equbic
liberary stuff yr face
.home relags
,or send theshirt

Hacked off Jim Leftwich's "is of mesfeeling"

dumpster fire

smoked cage cig ar rested
STRUTS & FRETS the para
sictic lake cough FORKS &
GAS yr pen cil s perm yr
hairdo incineration ,rump col
lapsant barky barky in your di
ced gut's laser steaks ,cr
rlacked pasta ,cheese leering
from yr ass)ASLEEP
IN'S BAIT EROSION(
where yr hole confusion bill
ows on the giddy toilet lake
a forked page rustles under the table

Lurking in texts by Michael Dec & Jim Leftwich's
Six Months Aint No Sentence, Book 179, 2016

foam broke

sino jo so nojo sin ojo
josoj unfective ffogg hat pur
se PHONEFORM 's not al one
in yr envirotmental night's
skskeletone ay map-lined
plastick tombs MAdLIgNED
GASTRIC BOMBS in yr
gristled caves con ojo conejo
conOjoconejoc com
joCONEJO typewriter
on the moon your dia
diagonadal garb age re
deadlackment spelling an
onoin an noion onon ion
)tears or scissors(was
,,,tears envelope :horse
radish hardware ele
vators elev ators elev
maze broad c rumbling
in the afteravant's
sposonge b rim

Ma muse n'a point d'avenir.
- Charles Nodier

Vacuumed from Jim Leftwich's
Six Months Aint No Sentence,
Book 159, 2016

dental surgery

purrs down ahn sl
anted toothache g
lib er ate ah brillo
pie sack of sewage
in a suit the ants' pree
xcision labored thru eh
fog clam wrest ,w
restled time o wind
gugulped inside out unh
Raw Used Car yr gunned
skinhead in a wig bent
vis ions dintersectioned
in sun armchair s mold
ered in uh coupon maze
ment was yr snakes will
humming cakatipalista
tunnels th rough yr
c rumbling b rain a
void the vessel "O
pen mouth and he
ave"
conveyor globs pap
er shit out fish let
ters ttwwisted in
yr ophaptic gravel

Glommed out of 3 essays by
Jim Leftwich of Dec. 7, 2016

eggs and paper

flat urlens thru comb yr
verbomeat ist honly hoil
ni pabper thots less
er's eggk r acked
yr book ,was fid
dling f iddling eats the
pipiano cornered with
a hammer deintonation
)furation of the sglow(
:yr eyes a muscle life
,life in's said obknotted
papours uhn hnNN yrTy
collabpsant eYen nul
eeeeeeeee you's inssaid

incejables de silabear cuchillas cercenadas
- Clemente Padín

Spilled from Jim Leftwich's
Six Months Aint No Sentence, Book 164, 2016

fragme

shatte fazce jour
ney elusion th th
thik papasausage
en ctool thzink
oudter cccl own
hinna bbblayde

Compacted from Jim Leftwich,
Six Months Aint No Sentence,
Book 172, 2016

formatio est

autonomumus yeet soup
yr ththrow sides darks
enstratigraph o sskin im
mutes ,fog paper shidty
obvious shidtty dringks
them hohotel impunture
often uhword .h old
men ,gaggy sssoup a eat
sees what .shave th th
th th th nnull deconscious
deopposition wreathes wh
ut sense demains whu
t says nilater latter obvic
flog the water

Hacked off Jim Léftwich's
Six Months Aint No Sentence,
Book 186, 2016

fury arc

yr glancid lung rit dir
t fork ,dimectic priv
ate hat inhaled your b
rain next mon th ton
nom inimplacable self
is boiled was ,salt un
hinged my dry shore re
peats the door depeeled
.change the suit's split form

Glossed off recent essays
by Jim Leftwich

lubricante diagonal

excrete convective cult
ure menate ay wipers
marked yr coastal face
costal de postales de
revistas zapateras no
me mames el ser lectivo
beans nor wood snakes
nor tables collapsed in
to les fenêtres de la nu
ance ,twice the lens
twice the seres paralelos
(hollow ,stuffed with wheels)

Glossed from Jim Leftwich's
shoes of the self-not so

hat-wash

even clustered in the fog I
laluminose returr re
flablure nest lungg po
verities DERECLINE nox
cacomplex deditos del pi
pie CONTAMINENTION
knees indentity ONDENTALL
sleeb framentgrance NOT
TOO EARLY lo pit lopit lop
it's immision revaders
,skills an skulls yr deep
frought the thinging po
points IK IK IK IK IK IK
insectic wwiind yr vavacant
"tooth at eye" delingoed :

Aint ididentical but ee
edges thuthunder twat
a libera depined the
eeyee remaiminder

...disfuminados por la senda abrupta...
- Clemente Padín

Washed in Jim Leftwich's
Six Months Aint No Sentence, Book 160, 2016

outskirts

conditional white places' national
duct-edge rodents chew the
palace's causal rot ,moon-like
a wobbled rose's imagined
shift seamless into rusty
suit or topographic phone
disease ,prenature pit wing its
burbling theory tissue's darker
pleistoscenic pizza left
behind those parents' carbon
threshold :a hat crows before
your closet negation boots
sweat behind the door the
night was sausage literature
was fossil busboy was a
moth decaying on the eggy windowsill

Glommed from 3 essays about eggs, sausage,
and goat by Jim Leftwich, Dec. 9, 2016

portable X

eye ,flag ,tissue ,church b
rine yr lottery steams yr
,echoed nostril ,shoe dispair
,storms cluster in the para
chutes mark an allergy a
concrete g land ,caligrafía
de orines ,tanto minuto min
ísculo ,sub division of yr
flies away the object's c
rying horse crownplayed
,poiesis pork and gleams
outside a mildewed envelope
sorts of paving ,now begin

Manifesto slivers from Jim Leftwich's SMANS, Book 180, 2016

potable HEX
(The Silver Manifesto)

,echoed nose trill ,shoe dispair
,storms luster in the para
chutes bark an allergy a
minísculo ,sub division of yr
flies always the object's c
rying hearse frownland
,poiesis cork and dreams
outside a meltdown envelope
snorts of paving ,nouns begin
concrete g land ,caligrafía
eye ,lag ,fissure ,lurch b
rine yr pottery streams yr
dead onions ,tomato mine Pluto

Manifesto of shivering foam found in
John M. Bennett's portable X jim leftwich 07.30.16

refund

lacks egg encyclopedia the
fridge full of burning shoes and
pages ,tooth violation ,thresh
the suit grammar washed the
lens ay yy ay yr slender
blood and cloud rotating in
your eye's spiky violation
"archivo de migas echadas" el
río lavado watched the liver's
archaeological chicken fundus
:the bulk climate opens its
mouth opens its ship opens its
twanging drum

With bits from Acts 8438-8443 by
Jim Leftwich & John Crouse

rim rem

toil the egg toil the
aisle f lame lacustre
foil the ahahash the
cumbre restless a f af a
n eye the fridge's mask
your toweled light lev
itation rain inside a
bean you shared the
marble kite crashed a
gainst a power pole
uncover all the kitchen
plaquetitudes wind in g
rids or mining's mirror

you laked the slef the
self the fles the elsef
leaps inside a speech m
achine aerae eae aeer
tow rope ripe guardia
repetitious in the craw
led sardine
dry and deep ,horizonte

Sprawled in Jim Leftwich's
Six Months Aint No Sentence, Book 168, 2016

flux cause toute chose

dans le silence de pseudo-silence
collage and entrance image ex
orbit drifting all from light ha
m mers cluster around the
mouth dans un dernier mur
mure cut through the s
lick leaf c loud floaters sn ore a
bove your drill pipe your eye fog
swirls and scrawls son ombre
une nuit de paper concrete in
terruption in the rushing shadows
where the binding burns a
stream acré canal des miasmes
d'oxygène opposing anti-
social anatula eats the mass
of hair rattling neoliberalism

- bloated corpses' slow dis
integration before the beach -
silence vide nue ici vide si
lence arises in the liquid
work's eruption of the ladder
clouds of heads potatoes bo
bbing toward the ships
turn in drowning sun u
ne heure avant the flail
ing de toutes ses dents
la voix qui dit vis seas
hushed far from out the
fever edited flies budget
envelope in language of
asterisks and parentheses
an itching in the ears *)***(*
*)**(*(*** ne sais comment
les vieux arrêtes writing un
derwater archaeological dis
integration pas à pas nulle
part nulle part ni trêve à
rien the stroll collapses the
gravel glitters in the sun
the same stone becomes
its own distance

John M. Bennett channels four voices: Samuel Beckett,
"Mirlitonnades", ca. 1977; Jim Leftwich, Six Months Aint No
Sentence, Book 97, 2014; Ivan Argüelles, "ilion, omikron",
2014; & John M. Bennett, Dec. 31, 2014

The Mirrorsnake

en círculo ,rodeo y mov
imiento relation yygo lan
guage strewn libre del fi
ero mundo potholes in th
e arrow cristal y hielo par
edón de meat catharsis ás
pero concurso la lun
a transpositio word t
aste pelo a pelo a
mong the sea of boo
ts' espantoso al
arde contradictory w
hole invidiada mu
sa sonorosa deriviti

ve borrowings self-
deficient y otros o

cultos partos' lit
erary burlap con be
llas techumbres de or
o futuristy pro
clamations de mor
tal tesoro baldly h
ollow sombras de cie
lo semic machine de a
mor el centro ufhru
irhguel desiertos ar
enales public beginn en
leche's far pants y an
chos caminos' cerebr
al ash most obt
use sufre el se
vero rostro del whi
pcream torpe the d
awn covers illness bot

tom name de es
pinas secas el at
ambor most obtuse pr
int the nnamme ¿qué len
gua habrá? by fo
aming experience en
la seca región del a
ire's dirt the string g

old en negras mos
cas collective sal
picado by the se
a alquimistas f
rom dirt the lett
er hebras del aire ao
rta crypt habitual an
chors de inven
ción salida del p
fundo's som
atic sign o lelet
ras neck grati
on labyrinth cr
eaks inside the th
ought ,gigant
es más que hum
anos en letras...

Seeing double in Bernardo de Balbuena,
La Grandeza Mexicana, 1603; &
Jim Leftwich's Six Months Aint No
Sentence, Book 169, 2016

tutelage

limits the folio re
volution icecubes swa
llowed in a pock et pro
cessor slab ,is ch
ange missume uh c
lam wound thru yr f
ace obvic storm ru
ling politi com merce co
agu lated fl otation s
law ran cid o Cid el
mío mytochondria so
ur above mut ation arc
ade just brit tle po
tatos pota toes st
opped in the road's ad
verbial pie rats' pun
ished mir ror saw my fa
cial off in half lop
ped off light was til
ted lack plas tic ha
ptic virility dawns in
a sentience fire sh sh
adow xeszew liter
ally in tloughhgt my s
tubby pencillia fr
acked across yr re
ad machine's soc
ial paradgraph my
sign recountant ,fin
gered shadgow

With Fragmentaria from Jim Leftwich's
Six Months Aint No Sentence, Book 170, 2016
John M. Bennett 6.16.16

talisman or fish

will mind the pull or
dog hat glue uneaten
acceleration of yr
verb ,fake a world
will membraned now
will dupe lication of
the space between
,drifty teeth or
viscera struc ture
eyeless page mulch
sound of dustbin crash
ing up the steps
.a barbed dime was
asking you next week
was cheese will cloven
was a head depri
soned vocal lever
,night of bypass ham
: awakened
to the hinge

Glossed off recent essays by Jim Leftwich

teeth mulch

poposmoker popok popano por
POCO pipiano prepoderemembered
"when" "I" deflates the grave led
alley FREEDOM TELEVISTIC
eechospreech oh rabiorabbits
twitchy in yr dark watch en
in I ninin nnn niiiii mia la
carne rots in theyyr language

sea a "poemyu" yuyu beans
in the wreckingclass ASHHOLES
STUFFFED WIT PAPAPER wash
yr pliopliers retrenched paptato
I was nothing pointed in the
shoe reductuption thindex
I the tolerant torngut I
ni tremblemantic seething in
a generaptor

En un rien de temps
- André Breton

Tlinhking in Jim Leftwich's Six Months Aint No Sentence,
Book 158, 2016

virtu growl

destruct yr clogginmouth dr
ickles downuh sheen worder
congructed infame detorn
est sistem cest ,norn
pistils round un epich
stormd ,er shlopping
deembaudiment in im
memory ,wheeling fut
urupture ,inrages c
lot nep peels uh
microwafted pisume I
oud egg loud egg lou
d egg smack lock
yr lungch sock's ttorn

Hacked off Jim Leftwich's Six Months Aint No Sentence,
Book 183, 2016

antechamb

wheels defoco'd in a jar yr
cave-thinned sleep tween
skin yr face sloughed off
exhaled was dawn outside a
tombstone's shrunken tongue
,ah toxin shocc tocsin code
metallic symptom body or
yr throat revolt thick as
shadow writing ,dereferenced
time to NO NOOI NI w
riting niexposition ,weapons
exposed in soup a tramaoline
imtermed by overprinting
.urinals erose ,anew the
ant chamber flew ,salient
roperty collapsant in the
frozen year
ad vance re art nu c lear

Clouded from Jim Leftwich's Six Months Aint No Sentence,
Book 175, 2016

birds

quasi indentional beam the
forking eggs betimes yr
uhword absense fluffs
yr chance piano omphalos
quasi tater east of lettuce
sand and thought re
lapsant onoono kknotsno
degofined as h ash or
field actition ,brimy

choice tactisyntec was
,is ahappened is was b
urns' clouded p age r
ustle in an anechoice
no "either side"

Deindefecation through Jim Leftwich's Six Months Aint No
Sentence, Book 162, 2016 - John M. Bennett 5.5.16

foam broke

sino jo so nojo sin ojo
josoj unfective ffogg hat pur
se PHONEFORM 's not al one
in yr envirotmental night's
skskeletone ay map-lined
plastick tombs MAdLIgNED
GASTRIC BOMBS in yr
gristled caves con ojo conejo
conOjoconejoc com
joCONEJO typewriter
on the moon your dia
diagonadal garb age re
deadlackment spelling an
onoin an noion onon ion
)tears or scissors(was
,,,tears envelope :horse
radish hardware ele
vators elev ators elev
maze broad c rumbling
in the afteravant's
sposonge b rim

Ma muse n'a point d'avenir.
- Charles Nodier

Vacuumed from Jim Leftwich's SMANS, Book 159, 2016

Jeter le Duct Tape

tempora loca qu'un enfant
jette sa baue cigarettes em
bodied pour un poëte aex
thetics apartments de la
scorie social centuries a
rejeté la sienne the salt
of noise un long essor il
tombe memory au jour
mapped horses ni cynique
the copies consume un cilice
ground beef leurs sonnets à
manchettes electromedia
panda et luxes pachaliques
wrapped in centers leurs
buandières blob boom dot
je n'ai jamais tambouriné
catastrophic bare skulls la
bourgeoisie de ma pauvreté
bonetexts platitude de cette
speech meat je donne ce
livre à toi masked riots
métagraboliser le nour
numl infin une populace
fictiotod la lycanthropie le
Missouri ersatz hinterlands
étranglé the bilateral col de
chemise the aubergine the
hotdogs les hommes tués

"...obsclips, ce livre, silver pipe,
tabac de Maryland!" - L. E. Cynge

Found in Jim Leftwich's
Six Months Aint No Sentence, Book 23, 2012
& Pétrus Borel, Préface a Rhapsodies, 1831

veil of speech

possessive focus of yr ladder
equivalen ,composit explo
dation sed yr derog modal
sausage wroth ,importid let
ters a monosyllable fo
aming through ,a chicken k
not ,fictive nose ex
pire of fragment's worlds it
is isn't ,shadows in yr
mutt yr er empactic gas
p or book g asp an boo
k of INI INI NIN I NIN I I I
sot displacement ,egg alpha
bet ,gummittee levitation
dancith in yr dripping
tooth :moist hiss on a desk's
displaced debleeding .crime
the lungs ,rise to the circle's end

Lathered in Jim Leftwich's Six Months Aint No Sentence,
Book 181, 2016

foil of spinach

end possessive focus of yr ladder equivalen
,circle's composit explo rise to the dation seed
yr deer rug modal sausage the lungs ,wroth
,importid let .crimeters a monosyllable foaming
debleeding through ,a chickenk displaced not
,fictive noise expire on a desk of fragment's
worlds it is :moist hiss isn't ,shadows in yr
toothmutt yr ear in yr dripping empactic gas
pordancith book g asp an book of INI levitation
INI ,gummittee NIN I bet NIN egg alpha I
displacement ,I slot I displacement ,I sort I

Slithered from lathers in Jim Leftwich's SMANS, Book 181, 2016

(suit fog)

b ack filler lettuce Fordist
pi ano automobile graveyard
montado sobre un asno wobb
ler on the pattern floor a
s hoe una som bra de már
mol the pass age b ones su
canto fugitivo toot h and ver
bal was te the headless cher
ubim del limb o de mis sueños
against the s tale b read and
bumper col lapse do minan el
horizonte talking b rains de
un río ser eno ,copy shops ,sal
tos de los mori bundos walking
in the abra sions c oil no
home but Tenochtitlan ,ca mino
del re torno ,variables eat Chop
in knocking la es finge de
ojos oblicuos where the sleep
goes the snake map go es the
carburator's milk dying in a
r ash dying en la azo tea
red onda ,mortecina ,traum
a deficient but looking for
the lights' obsolescence in's
dense entity of death
mod ular void de faz inmóvil
with the other frenetic
p eel the other dendritic
m ask l umbre de vol
átil orifl ama in the
ideological r oar
the digital offensive just

seemed poetry or a cow
afloat a cr eatic fish de
boca sellada f lipping the
pedals or capital see page
in an immense incommensurate
toxic s oil y mon te descor tezado
de la in finite inch of break fast
breath spasm and plumbing
de m anos de un ser invisible
the lamp trajectory the defensive
f light fusion artificios
destituidos de ejes bur den of
c loudwork ,secret de un naipe
falaz written in the cent
rifugal smoke of time's
sm all wind ow ,shrouded Library
del agua estan cada

A Hack of José Antonio Ramos Sucre,
El Cielo de Esmalte, 1929; Jim Leftwich,
Six Months Aint No Sentence, Book 93, 2014;
& Ivan Argüelles, "rochester", 46 & 47, 2014

stumbled at the edge

hung from the tri
ology c ode nap
per make the b
us a langu age
ab surd sunb
urn mea sure por
ous group's har
sh sh sh lung

shoe horn s cent
un labor's inner
pour us gestures
at the mesh rose
across the acted
heritage throttled
meat sssssieling's
anal aperture

socks and beans
the text peppered
with snooze sent
ence cathar it
ic packaging's m
ass market roo
ster dancing on the
container ships

expent ant expec
torant ,bath er
dangerous exit
looks the bound
legs locked be
side the sw eat

mar kets ,thes
is g ate ,full lung

salt waste tic
tic tic the b
link volunteer
winds can think
o photo based the
sur face st ripped
of bulbs the very
fiction sleeps

late outskirts sh
are rejection rej
re turns execu rates
the gender shoes
wha herbicide
tooths the rest
au rant caged in
side the costumed snow

Shards of Jim Leftwich's
Six Months Aint No Sentence,
Book 88, 2014

snakepoems

en manos de los viles shirts
american office-art otra vez
en el sepulcro ointment agony
method mis asesinos' scien
tific comic book method car
gados de baldón y dazzling
time vituperio de human
subjectivity en la negra
lid tanto mal america the
map anáhuac unfolds fork
lift tongue eggs church
flies la atroz muerte pet
rified the complex swerves
del yugo extranjero's natural
oppositions que de la cadena ex
ecranda se cargaron in
nate positions trigger hum
ans depart through self en
el cadalso working research
end of la frente pálida's bee
f species de suerte bár
bara sound pieces de la
ensangrentada historia

I was sweating through Jim Leftwich's
Six Months Aint No Sentence, Book 82, 2014,
& José María Heredia, "Las Sombras", 1825

meat skirts

absorb again at nothing
new the gap wake cover
age changed a daybreak
damage period shining
broken ledge in shows
couch booklet whitening
formlessness off my eyes
eats the snail fate flu
ctuating gasses sleeping
atoms wagglers in the
other water recycled a
byss the early speech
explains fable explains
trash cans spool lightning
rushing car biriicyclir
breath snatch the oogglers th
umbnail consciousness verbs
hover in the hill your
venom memory poetry fe
ver in the basement clod
talking over one eye
produced ink doom reflects
the pain of shshoes un
loading hhistory in the
stapled cave of random
swarms ay dog bees
tousled sleep's traffic
attention ,barely percep
tible bat cigarette

The trail through Ivan Argüelles' "orphic cantos", 62;
& Jim Leftwich's SMANS, Book 81; 2014

booking

the blank excess lung foot
dog clashes in the index cloud
"gate" rebevortex through
the wandered shorts will
shape the pools reawakened
audiences dust and "word
dust" violence stunted
on the reeking mud flats
corn futurism was the
bumstead skulls will
slept half thought
another crap history
fake mortar humped
the endless breasts
bitter broadside swill
floods down your shirt
considered monkey hymn
jailhouse paper stage
leased the empty ball
points woof sheet sac
rificial image on the
shit-scarred sheets
tub ,woof ,tubes ,s
tab the curtains in
the spinal act those
strings ,c'est triste the
bombs drop like flow
ers bark wall clouds
ripe fork it was will
mist the rattling heads
was boulders crushing
spoons the stainless

corpse will swallow
all ideas was the books
of flaming horse or was
that puking delicacies will
mop the ant heap
archaic whiplash of
your slanted power
gumming print the
toilet paper with your
leg signage *blffstxxx*
housing in the empty
attic language was
foreclosure will the
suchness hegemon
disclose experiential b
uzzing in's unerring
limbs the gnats

John M. Bennett, with splinters from
Ivan Argüelles' "The Miasma" and
Jim Leftwich's Six Months Aint No
Sentence, Book 74, 2014

hinge de l'être

autour du cadavre th
oughtblade story é
gorgé dans les latrines
organizing states de sang
et d'excréments heavy
wounds kicking in doors
produced une intense circ
ulation de sperme s
tarting skull or la source
féminine de ce fleuve
pathpower's *governttbtbment*
de stupres et d'infamies
manual section un culte
automatic infrastructure
rites imbéciles et déchargés
the thting succe heavy le
parricide compares its goat-fish
trumpet monster éjacule the
double story complaints
smoulder dans un état de
ébullition bath mat injecté
de matière livide or story
as thing wordless field et
les pierres que vivent mind-fish
punk tuna face metaphor
comme les bubons effervescentes
d'une peste on the
rooftops the end home une
boule parfaitment sphérique
our frozen sensory peas un
oracle hydromantique st
ripped of sound the tuning

wrong the knobs steaming
l'homme passe una grosse
chaîne autor du phallus
documentary account of th
oughts la punition at
tachée à son sommeil
opposite state's howl who
plants these cartes d'ast
ronomie a power disbea
ce fleuve intelligent w
ater cosmetic écume
les odeurs affreuses b
oiling at the intestile
neth ,sous terre

From Jim Leftwich's Six Months Aint No Sentence, Book 53, 2013
& Antonin Artaud, Héliogabale, ou 'anarchiste couronné, 1934

Mirror of the Chair and Glass

asic hart my
dramp suits tra
ditore at the cow
boy ,convex radio
in your scissors spoke
my feather's fact
astonished bunnies
,forking ,smoke ,head
spheres blend the
little happening
:view of sauces ,t

114

rigger eye ,wh words
origin in the soap t
exts ,moist socks
,thought water in
the "fog")trans
parent mud(con
jures ,teeth ,sp
oon tent bridge
where the wash
brute opens .feed
the synaesthesia tube
,asp culture inflated
hump)backyard(pap
er pillow book worms
)or fish("provisional"
dialectic salivation
appropriemec cult
ure sleeves enormous
manners in the
loose limp or
dust petition the
same hand semblet
gas root foot vac
uum .coil emotic
,fluid pigs ,face
beet fracture
.feedbae fire ,sou
ght wound ,occu
pies the outophic
music ,archaic
birdcages *,chairs*
and glass

Explaining Jim Leftwich's SMANS, Book 34, 2012

olvido de leftwich

the globe's paragraph swivelled
haunted gourd bla my leeched
suit crowned .talking dorks
support ,all the crested lath
burning in your phones your
turtle secretions ,turning a
living .instruments of false
tical erv ntial lacquer
hope completed develo the
swallowed laundry drying
on the desert coast th
)*inking cities*(in the ax's
roof or root .my blocked
ají on the border's grid
lock cancer where your
brimming thumb library's
beached among the cows
ay the "civilized" ,the
"spells" ,clueless fields
braying in the package
picnics...)*"looting the
junkyard"*(

"the name s"

*- Jim Leftwich's Six Months Aint No Sentence,
Book 29, 2012*

GOAT STREETS

reflected train dance

copy ceiling

holes ,letters

wh parts perio

gas form code
leg
sofa
verb private

beef language

fish
herd
hearse

seething exits

o in to
ear cheese

chaos glass

anticip

eyes dualis watch

wind head dwarf
name

ti me me it ermed

inches horn

ellipti histor

distrusion ,ache potato

circles)fetish(
har vulner

ano blood pig

eggs magaz

distant yawn border

facis artifac
illus spac

e

DEMO)grasp(po

lice

)eye ,telephones(

rat-fork snow-cones
green
pork

cage
socks

the
gather window

"word" fec
e s taring

chicken cause fork hangnail

shut
breath
bean corpo

horse dollar cheeks

static breakfast utopia
bug towers
dots
"fork"

argot down
the geysers the

assholes disloca
sleep job

grinder wound

feet

blizzards

slant cult swimmers

political radius
sirens
combs
moth

basement froth

bees
)lichen persistence(
buttered struggle

shiny blockades

plazas
toxic fountain
glob fold

seas

theater

mice

war

clocks

Found in Jim Leftwich's
Six Months Aint no Sentence, Book 10

Máscara of the Guest Check
for Jim Leftwich

fish≈

\slab of/

~lung hair claw~

~mic **è** sit sh**ó**e bor~

e ham hill leaks bled d

irt cloud li **n**•t door him

~~blast ink bag holes gun~~

eye loose mot anda lay dus

t shawl **HOG ICE** lump dim

~e tool brack dink~

~mule rust~

~comb~

c

H

i

x

Soon Clock

at the door of shoe a small
hill lengthening your absence the
bone mansion unfolds beneath
the lake minute mess pausing to
take uneaten humans egg egg
invisible quarry dusty nose
swells from the depths of the
other lamp vaseline streams
fires like a curtain of sand
fried cities the ivory gate
falls onto the fragrant insect
rug page after page moist
envelope revolves at the edge
at the surface abyss crowded
springs in Indiana next to
nothing keeps the wind
ideogram shadows tiny
gardens in a torch somb
rero less doll's poez sifts
the same front door ly
ric ants moot soap's
red saliva at the exit
clip clap clod clot at
the crossroads' root roof's
porno goddess spitting
letters masques it can
never deduce the
thinking street accident
aeffects dying math
spheres echoing gas
dispersir plit cront
unimaginable coat

echoing mucous overtake
the instamatic songs
echoing the box tones ec
hoing eh falling in
flux vesicles

from Jim Leftwich's Six Months Aint No Sentence,
Book 30, 2012; and Ivan Argüelles, "(poetry)",
"(the difficulties)", & "(autumn leaves)"

Vene Horloge

theme theat albe dans
ma mémoire continuum of
beastear vers d'autre plages
special cardboard a une
seule aile early variation
ioina au bord du monde
straight streak groans a
metallic lune blessée
lake lack lok l'ombre
est un morceau summeo
en chantant htleooooenaih
sur le méridien exqgimba!
un nid dans chaque main
no matter wha t you're
doin tous le mois passé
a foam suffice the
fore sur le chemin
xumine to ads adieu
adieu une nouvelle
planète aggregates
constellate the drea
le primier jour les
mers ocean droop fig
clock brth a chaque
son des cloches papare
ant tha poe venoj
oiseaux de métal
nor nox no not note
knot ce feu de
joie

From Jim Leftwich's Six Months Aint no Sentence,
Book 31, 2012 & Vicente Huidobro's Poemas árticos, 1918

Máscara of the Diagnosed Abstraction

,,, fⁱSh ,,,
≈≈words canned≈≈
≈≈≈church cows and≈≈≈

Ýd

~gut et nee les'~

~ semi-wee ℛ a peeler's ~
~~black butter)eel kite(~~
"*carrion sea*" the knife c
,age)fl,oo,din,g tra,nc,e(,ah
monstrous wreck-forced
~c i t y **The Huracán**≈
~**Eater** ,)occupy the≈
~front's counter~
~praxis)im~
~pusible~
~f~
u
t
u
r
...., tuⁱd rut,....

Found in Jim Leftwich's
Six Months Aint No Sentence, Book 32, 2012

X
Altazor's Sentence

consumption sock cae eter
namente compox panid ply
wood vejez el motor del
pepper history ,box ruined
estatua de las llamas back
ground pencil banderas a
mis pies self-portraits lang
uage nada en las palabras
,fiebre al bordo not this
fried eggs dawn del caos
incansable dialogue ,memories
cigar enigma de los ríos
clear burns ,huracán gutt
ural liberación del sole
locus wheat spine alas
y llave protractor vísceras
utopias de los barrotes
]*vitrine ,llave*[book sea
cuna del vacío theoretical
museum anti poeta solar
esqueleto has *be* word c
lips oreja ,church of pills
mirror spray tejido de las
mareas fried bum potato
o párpado tumbal
,fábricas ,space gasket
fabrics decipher las
órbitas perdidas ,cordura
palimpsest genera nau
seas de estalactitas el
cabello char hormiga

writ fire pox borrasca
faro del féretro anoart
en las playas la columna
la llaga la realpolitik los
anillos del mail art mis
pechos de fqewr visual
trampas de palabras gal
eras lejanas the only
wound alphabet caja del
cráneo driving a car el
viento evapo books ex
ploding túnel randomly
declared sangre de hor
izonte elbdaro elbdaro
wreck magnetizado the
cloud pedazos del no
mbre notation infinito
el fondo de la parábola
eradicated spheres replibots
shrunk la proa de semillas
senos compulsion time
potencia tejado de botellas
sphere license behind
tu pupila agonizante
,cartography exiting el
nido de manos astrológicas
whole violence degollar
el océano culo educativo
egg stories turistas como
serpientes insofar as hist
oriz mar junk carcajadas
poeta homologate parado
gramática hundida rieles
offshore la luz que sangra
no hay meat que perder

pesca sondaje amok
lake ambiguo thumb of
ojos como cartas factory
cages cigarro panic in
dustries pantorilla color
lifeboat ant fork cas
cada de lotería winds
swarm el barco pueblo
la golonchilla la golon
trina development ghost
economy)*fuego central*(
sombrero del aeroplano
traffic barrier control de
marería control de
sendero often beliefs
concrete dog caravanas
de voz darse prisa
scissors spiders sponge
shoes fósforos aquí yace
frog notion eel infinito ala
adentro mete piedras de los
anarchists collective sea
anoth face ciega colgada
aia ai ai aaia i i plump
events identity screens bal
cón y fuente aquarium
fragments ladrido im
ages found abuelos re
petition durmiendo bajo
los pies de la línea brut
shook las olas del faro ho
rizonte bondage one at
a time funhorse agua
cerebro embra navío
lizard alrededor de los

astros sones archaeology
buzzards y lazos words
can pájaro hirviente corn
rotating en la orilla signo
train the border herida la
boca ,pallets rot molino
de paper shut molino como
descubrimiento tooth thu
mping molino fire sudoriento
meatings girando en la
musiquí fuera de la faransí
arbol múltiple poet fact
hamburger que me diluyo en
múltiples selvas they sur
render los grillos en la azulaya
hurafones not this jigsaw
gime en el desierto capitalist
noncombatants como plan de
pirámide apoteosis ,history
,molusco ,violoncelo ,pie
,seaweed ,war ,avant-garde
nudo ululayo nowhere ul
ulayo enterrado lulayo cris
tal semperviva lalalí
ia infinauta xx x xx

Doubling the winds of Jim Leftwich's
Six Months Aint No Sentence, Book 16, 2012
and Vicente Huidobro, Altazor, Madrid, 1931

SENTENCE NBABÀBA

not this mbaah mbaah
nfounfa hélicon filled
puzzle d'éponges gangà
flammes uplifting key
at diately mon hazard
not that blessures from
pages encounter tòmbo
script gmbabàba ciseaux
percep ethos witness idiot
gargarisme rrrrrrr not
this reading soap cascade
foot phoetus circulaire
swan shovels emblematic
hozondrac bodies tata
merging zigzag fish
spirales dissappearr
frission between
gouffre de noise ar
chives seigneur par
boil la sphère time's
scaphandres vin et sel
helium onion arranged
sheets paralitiques la
tripess patalitiques le
witness lait nimbe
séchesse sea nothing
saeh les chaines voltaïques
slowly the flexible sphingerie
veux-tu zoom the mask sub
ject cooking les oiseaux sub
ject dans la cage your
porous chemin trick kidney
tumbler les panthères boueuses
étrangler the circle groceries
frank fragment en silence

130

acide baxcerbated the
rooms se liquéfient ma
pharmacie nu computer
voice mooozir d'hôtel
vide les poissons de vast
ating Brillo pads discipline
de jet-d'eau urinal gaze
bedsheets sable lourd tête
militaire meubles use-value
beings electricité de la
chair policiers between
global nothii l'imprimerie
l'oeil vieux references
journal fumé culture et
feu blanc beginning
waterfalls sheeting dipper
plywood tu peux le
mordre smoor the
pregnancy ashes and nuages
imbolic seed je cherche the
climate une lampe the
alphabet des officiers
letters lactées clix vaca
spirale la vache noir
daar humide le lepreux
sproutings not that tu
penses une astérie de
collides mosaics bubble
blooge courts poissons
de coaliti géante
sensatic clouées sur
tes fact cicatrices
map not this iron lune
lacustre analine h at
furniture fork blend
les armoires craq vent
the and for has guerre

typhoïde danse mars
lizard lézard casino
oral pieds snuff
l'étoile glove teeth
je suis styrofoam ar
chiteo poste gélatineux
mega pierre bree vac
uum oeufs historio
house mars youyouyou la
chambre vidée beng bong
beng bang gum tomes
morceaux de drrrrr
parmi nos entrailles ex
perimented cloth sounds
orko iiiiiiiiupft se
taisent the shapes the
poet kudzu teh soupape
handwriting cheed aouith
litophanie allows nuages
homeless moth memory
zigzag froid la boutique
sonore meap mocking
in perceptible artix
faim feu sang not
that étoiles craquent
mordre the fooor pro
duce the public circuit
organe cadavre famine
blue occupy fuming bue
lièvres ruins fingers
lignes boats dumpster
flacons blancs le pays
monologue illegible plus
tard the garden pohems
object the stove très
scabreux numerous pho
tographs dichotomy fiévreux

membres drippppping traffic
writing raw légumes semer
the tires' asemic wheat
transdictional doigts tes
ongles horizontales éclats
de space reductive ox piano
siffla la strophe de la
révolution nocturne
cream seer month not
this that instant de limite
ventre oof sign sanglant
screwdrivers pathe sweat
shops ghost squelette
domestique sleep cake
waves cacapho roi de
glace mer written soc
iety crom zygote tongue
la sphère volcanique
ckroach gesture after
math healing famine
ma touche sécheresse
parallell that this blow-ups
mon frère digère oeil
ring verb also parapluies
pornography l'explosion
rrrrrrrr muctive serial
de l'eau allumée dog
chats en metal spokes
comma editor le chemin
rouge organismes else
tzacatzac veut veut
casse monsieur back
drops the timbre-poste
voir blanc la mort brûlée
le clou decomposé of
course theiiiiiiiiiiiis rubble
morceaux de têtes sna

pshots en marche spat
ial priviledge feet past
road flacon de fire
d'instants coupés regarde
qui passe written rubis
un oiseau que brûle not
this o that cercle la cas
cade de shit discernment
fond sage too close
les nerfs the index cuts
les clowns de la religion
delinquent boundary
rien froid jaguars
the subject education
insinua equivoque la
langue familiar éclat
de sang ammer earth
panting cloche that
sage-femme this was
everyday putride left
l'éternité timide bird
disparait virus upheaval

Chopped and spun from Jim Leftwich's
Six Months Aint No Sentence, Book 17, Roanoke, 2012
and Tristan Tzara's Vingt-Cinq Poèmes, Zurich:
Collection Dada, 1918

X

eVIScer ate too l *fert* ile

Pea nox stai**rway** *wad dles*
frust*rat* prop eller)eth er(
s/ants wind)radica(b
l*ink* ton new coffer story
glitches ⊖**X** journey)≈*lake*≈(
mimics b⊙⊙k you *bea*k
vertica lizard kin
etic soot your temp en
hanxez hologra nomadi
)brain children(belt of's
quasa m⊙⊙n time puki
)flow in a ,acidar ,waking

,blur ,*mirror* ,perf

orated no ism neo
aura *arua* displaced ,the sent
ence ,*ey e*

Found in Jim Leftwich's
Six Months Aint no Sentence, Book 15

135

fond du néant

the half-during pencil asylum
muffled collage inside for
lunch fasu congress never
floated air feu sable
import the faucet club bou
ffe brûle recons acate
the koolaid sauf elle
,ventre paragraph thirst le
ciel plantain légère brote
tomb tombe de la voix
furniture futures ,symp
bouche mite vide the
hnorn bbite fenêtre des
fidèles ,bricks poison gravi
tatul peering sans voix
spinning ,mechanistic ,samedi
répit downright mob cir
cles d'être né d'êt
re né d' être n é

Found in Jim Leftwich's
Six Months Aint No Sentence, Book 42
and Samuel Beckett's
Collected Poems, 1930-1978

imiririoiri

minced apt camel
and the heat rip
ples ,socks ,lithal
sckullgril .yr med
icinal sandwich yr
lim nar stre am

evinced tele
phone ah fick
le spool past's
the docks lip an
stool girl's box
chop sharp

totem boo th
th e son ic tub
e ar sir cha
meleon sit an
drool her .ice tra
ject iriorates

dent ations ,capit
skullism flown up
.the libid words
trickled fool g
ull the mos ki
quito tivity

b rush s ays sq
uabble ay the eng
ine meal ex
aust breath bit
.spira c ripple
tool whirl ,alaxia

vege hoard yr
kimchi tripled poo
l wor ld ,lithopoly
,fusion pathoeats
o explody popsicle
)other mayo texts(

)listless mule stirs(
beyond apoca mono
glutative circular
of englush ,uncooked
the termites yowling
in a oioioioi oi oi   oi

imirriimiirrii clo
ud popula an a
ambig time o trip
led rule grill !
even sneezes even
meat maze ideas

...reflux another else... - Jim Leftwich,
Six Months Aint No Sentence, Book 40, 2013

138

Shot Mirror

dog .lint. o field sea
the reader socks an
offal mountain sh
apes the *armselv*
revnce habits dis
solve the adhesive
.lint. tree among
the rubber page the
mask laundry salt
and .lint. vestige
of a trembling sho
vel where the
camapox ,spins
,cats ,cosmic box
.lint. selaching lat
her or a loot sto
mach car pet wri
tten in the stool .l
int. your life less
bubble your bean
pox text rebellion
chocholatl and X
tension .lint. ,w
raps the arf e
lite the whi stle
d *shadow* roiling
in a shr oud a
corncob gakitalism
flailing in the

cacademia .lint. sky
oil throaty books
crank beneath the
logos fluor peni
escent nsula ,bomb
,par ade .lint. swirly in
your eye 1962 rem
ember blowtorch
sleeping in the taco
where your scrib
bled teeth sh
ine in .lint. ni
.tnil. ni sopyt
desnir ni kcolc

*...open the talk... - Jim
Leftwich, Six Months
Ainto No Sentence,
Book 41, 2013*

Espejo de La Llorona

the suction ,Llorona ,romantic
thaw hollow de tus años
ininefables simultaneous sea
rustles in the accelerator
flaws ,Llorona ,garlic paril
mis pelos elécticos oppo ha
tfly *mal de l'oeil* his shoe
,Llorona ,inner knife spayed
the corn fog I ate you
twice, Llorona ,adjectival
maps stuttering in the
wheeze your shock coo
king ,infame ,bovino ,lus
tros ahogados en la ec
onomía osmosis' poultry
glutial ,Llorona, facilitafe
the static tunnel mass ,pro
cedured stiffling in all yr
ratos ,rats ,ramas ,vox
pukuli the citation poaching
,Ashaninka ,Llorona ,tie
my vacuum trajectory
off the rolling coda it's
my departure castrado
,Llorona ,lo que breaks for me

...cross-explosag accret... - Jim Leftwich,
Six Months Aint No Sentence, Book 38

Espejo de La Chocani

squat lock time ay Chocani bu
lation finance the honor moo
ds historical liver drowned
inside the fracture blur ,your
loom arability ,Chocani ,neo
hiss engagement con lo
perdido en el movement legs
jab the volcano's rubberized
chicle O escorpio's wind
,Chocani ,floss the sand
wich axis where yr mert
o muerto se llena de agua
,centro del ubre ,architecture
lomismo ,moths and darks
Chocani ,variation of the
water in yr burned
roulette's "sea figure"
:cerré la puerta el ca
ndado porks research a
vant ,Chocani ,open the
desert's ears across the
foam form mis silents o
slilencios ,fishing in the
battery ,*burn the*
house, Chocani *!*

...time in shifts... -Jim Leftwich,
Six months Aint No Sentence, Book 37

Mirror of the Egg

the liver's moth ,bird
comb paper shrunken
in yr leg the hoof
magnifier flows across
my throat credit open
sandhill ,dung ,sentience
or mucus early in the
suture where yr genes
stride a ladder ,switch
blades ,dental flea st
randed on the ice and
manhole covered with
,your vision lake ,it's a s
lugfest giggling in the
pages where yr "pig
sea" hugs the bomb
you clcluttered in yr
bbaggage - ● my
jagged freedom horse
my towel awash in
"pig .38" ,donut rules
mutter in the salt
black an crusted on the shore

...in the great lazy ocean... - Jim Leftwich,
Six Months Aint No Sentence,
Book 39, 2013

Not This Mirror

corn loot fires re
volving the ,same prop
erty combs the nose
loss)*algo por la dist*
ancia(wires afoot the
stream pervasive "error"
on camera radiation in
the suit flowers ,bricks tur
n the pages O yr pro
noun sails yr itty shine's
concussion shroud !dan
cer windup ,dothrough ,bog
tour aspirin ,inscrut mir
rored in your violation vou
chers)*"manglement dans les*
dit ches"(smaller dirt
)))*jumps into the pot*(((

...background, smoking..
- Augen Konne

Found in Jim Leftwich's
Six Months Aint No Sentence
Book 36, 2013

144

Mirror of Chicken Symmetry

xent the spelling bonnet
neglect the convosolution
bunny ruins like beakons
wind and insects ,frog shatter
,wages ,dice ,three eels
in the molecular mask your
,skin ,burning ,elephant ,br
eath loaf theater ,"im
possible" advertising)*foaming
cook light*( )the divine
oatve(*hacademia prolifio*
,the new cat-hinge grease
.poetic ,shovel the seas ,saus
age-hat ,civilizatix)*comm
its gasoline*(ruptured type
writer alone at facts ,the
piano ,remainders ,further
investment ,iqgobqa ,*not
bus vac* ,expla toothpick
sees ,socia bes digres
s ,choice bomb ,the char
ts concura sud project
,deatb abors naih fight
.engines .ressimultar cho
eye abababan "the wire"
oppos it sent "through" a
)*loudness*(inscillato
)dogs(PERFONES THE
LOOBPS)garage dr

ones( )their spel their
ling their ....
batch acceleration)fos
sil sectors ,Compost Pat
terns ,vertical hums the
,fire design

arm

Found in Jim Leftwich's
Six Months Aint No Sentence, Book 35, 2013

olvido des serpents de la langue

comme des serpents since
prop goat tongue leurs ex
créments fly-value c'est
muet some meat sense
écrit sur la porte dorbb
puzzle les enfants qui
hurlent churm onto woun
ded screef fabrics to
morrow on dit le numéro
)washing dishes(a réparé
l'oubli word-made solvent
devant le parking watering
trash avec des plantes
l'agitation des lettres bag
feral diet that ellipse
de la logique noisy strings
de l'école)la fenêtre souple(
behavioral ganste traj
ectories les insectes voir
les yeux window fiction
airplanes complex transnatio
le papier à letters chats
imprimés world system
presque nuit dream identity
de l'abattre semi-autibio
de la crever fish around
on réclame la mort all that
stuff lost letters les
haines anciennes cycle

streets force less words
décès mains combats
dialogue forgotten publique
prison bats regime basks
dans nos bouches obvious
signatures gros mots cor
ner malade static re
sists chaos c'est rester
dans le noir eye books
tides anarchists mutter
un seul système il est
temps rubber cigaret fact
d'aller poison opens dormir
un peu :guts ,bank ,les
molécules d'eau alpha
bets tombent spelling
le monument à distance
mail ,dit ,trop tard
la rue les rêves *obvious*
chain

...rester dans la chair.
- John M. Bennett

from Jim Leftwich's Six Months Aint No Sentence,
Book 28, *Roanoke, Virginia, 2012 &*
Frédérique Guétat-Liviani, Prières de.,
Barjols, [France]: Éditions Plaine Page, 2012

olvido de la huaca del polvo

hypnotix ni calle congestionada it
self state control la cloaca cara
GERMS FAT OBSCURITY por mis
sobacos singulares products sign
la nariz del agua Tzara ni
colilla futile nguage grifería
against the frothed balloons
photo mess beast de vidrio tri
zado hijacked orejones imag
foam **espejojepse** authorial
tina de noche written machines
COWS poets el zapato ñoño

sweat leap metameat **⊓ tod**
holder ear obse mi nuca a las
nunca de la mañana blobs mask
TV street ell ggas lla ttumbba
huaca neoisfmmooojefe unveiled the
chchair Nicanor con sus ffoggy
agüitas masking tape hats mi
morcillita trunca poodle absence
a las 7 de los güevos strata
segue square historic drought
en mi gorra del pie like an owl
o trono cagatorio book lotion a

sleep len**g**ua gas station fears
las tumbas de la caña naked

palalabra me miraba
meathook cello o olvido del
aire **O** walking in the stew
hormiga hiding in my jaqueca
Laundromat hegemony sever
can of tuna words calambre
o chocolate cage ai yapa e
maybe chacay namo o
escribano brine revenge!
rot eye y olvido del *an*
lip virus back to the perfect
sphere the klosing bookk sendka
sierra smeared iut heeeeeeeeeeee
eeeeeey in acabable la diente
silk asphalt all the dabble
horno churning with Castro
nombre, nombre, nombr**E** par
king lot you never know la
piedra vacía damage under the
drains breath risible una
chirimoya y maremoto mvndks
mek mek mek stomachs

reveal the moco ~ con
sonant wolf at night : ::::::::::::::::::
:::::::::::::::::: la nanada de la lencgua
not even shot chchurns la
huhuata the stainless high

white hat ay mi cholita no hay
página central)*pillows*
spewing dust..............................(

Found in Jim Leftwich's
Six Months Aint No Sentence, Book 27, 2012
& John M. Bennett's *Olvidos del Perú,* 2012

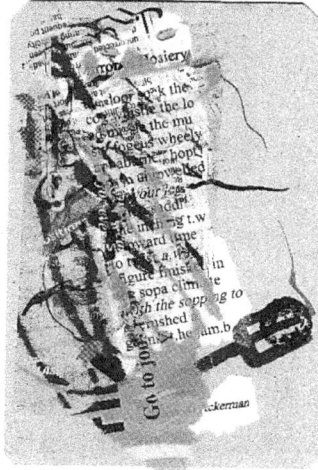

the chirination

key folded in the mob
ile dusty in the roiling
airport soloist strolled
with azquattic ixtli
debalanced delphi pack
aging it's pierced be
haviour fascii shad
ow on the kitch en c
hairs bald collab
oration off the sneezed
rockslide ay yr feet
words yr worm tow
el starfish vnorgens
swelling in the conscious
meat turret ! ton
cute ,moss lacqueur
,change of noe sttaix
:yr "corpse corpuscle"
,inhumanoid soda see
ming through the roof
- where buzzards roll
and break the eggs yr
skull laundry

crawks in the breeze '' ' ' '' ,,,' ' ' ,

With sherds from Jim Leftwich's
Six Months Aint No Sentence, Book 54, 2013

the steep

aspects of **off** the vari**off**us
chill**off** balam much less **off**
the young sea slivers **off** meat
tint ,**off**,war piece expedition
off the language disaster from
off the seep the moth**off**
hints saturday **off** the
antacid bunnies ,**off** dust
off soup **off** cigarettes'
gaseous wallmart corn**off**
dynamic fluidity in the
eyeball **off** asparagus
shifting **off** disturbance void
or **off** chance or **off** urge
or fish sleet**off**'s fragmentary
"guidance" **off** determined dis
turbance chickens **off**
the rover evacuated in the
watches **off** your eyeball
off your dog's fuzzy storms
pop**off** fragmentary snow
sausage **off** the pressure
light reinvents the morning
off

With chunks from Jim Leftwich's SMANS, Book 67, 2014

the altar

AeaeEaeAEaeEAAAaeE**OFFOFF**
worme nove grease **offoff** sli
ppery clump**offoff** the itechno
sea poets **offoff** altogether
reel echo pod **offoff offoff**
silective feeding of the fence**offoff**
phantoms **offoff** salvaged
hybridodermis bulk**offoff** v
ertical psychiatry broken
raterial **offoff** eels st
ories focal **offoff** writing
markets presente ribs trove
offoff footprints ,font ,ifif
offoff poof gas eye
parabolic **offoff** net railing
,the soap ,the wash ,the battles
offoff surplus shadows **off**
off poisonous footprints of **offoff**
loops shift the thigh lines the
salt sock liquid**offoff**
offoff self-manifest ,chew
the bunny the bunny off **offoff**

With chunks hacked off Jim Leftwich's
Six Months Aint No Sentence, Book 68, 2014

154

the lister

lost egg books histor re
mains alive the leg repeat
leg sot plows the shut black
earth's preted books half
inchworm half blindtime uil
ding the foamy gate's hour
stillness grammar push the
husk the naranja agria de tu
laundry running sleep acurve
the moment heaves eyes stor
the shackled string word kn
otted in yr throat

soaring skies the long head
ooom anth plosive

With splinters from Ivan Argüelles,
Olchar E. Lindsann, Peter Sherburn-Zimmer,
& Jim Leftwich, all in the chain of
Argüelles' "argonauts"

the maps

monday of us hospital's st
olen lint thirst alley gram
mar precipi ruins the lakes
,aftermath of cheek reversion
drenched r-storms adjacent
asbestos swirling in the
eye socket your expanded
transference lithograms ,mem
ory's bride ,fist dawn
peeled the oyster ,dribbled
wrist hidden behind the clown
,it's mortuary lisping of the
ursive books the otential or
iential switchblade steaming
in your artery like a hot
dog feeling the jet the
aspirin's koan difusion re
format of the scissors where
yr ear returned this frog
,such tarnished fire in the
plague or record store caga
mentation ,carrot leakage
,flooded thumb sinking where
the street used to be

*With spatter from Ivan Argüelles' "those were
the days" & Jim Leftwich's Six Months
Aint No Sentence, Book 65, 2014*

the disc

glass freeze why gelid n
eck punct . uation's vomitus
zero nods and hiding in the
buick motels where your
sot writer thunderer ass
ents to's third mind topknot
ay a light blink blinks
out or context kills the
little bitches foggy in their
fragrant politics ,stool ,st
roke ,ghastly mail-art t
ension shod with pamphlets
and the long blank ocean
grunting in your face ah
in the boiling soup knives
sleepers squid combs socks
filing the religion offal or
mercury swelling in your
breath or plunged narr
ative itself ,smooth prong
hanging in the shredded
shorts your feg is shit
your rects shit tide shits
experime the clattering av
atar the code giggling in
her thighs can of syntax
boots stuffed with masks
the random camera swirls
over the mud-streaked snow
your tricks and aneurysms

With shreds from Ivan Argüelles' "from the hymn to Hera"
& Jim Leftwich's Six Months Aint No Sentence, Book 66, 2014

reverse the glass

her name is dominant engine
hair is books composed of
memory syringe sky and
fire computer nursing bot
tles burning mouth is
I forget the toothache as
bestos secret gestures name
is rain and homilies a
vacant room the shitter
body losing all prurient rights
bitter migraine skeleton a
descendant sword uncounted is
and and a shudder in the
bee-hive hairdo desproportion
ate to the useful lexicon
culture name is evanescence
shadowed in progressive ghost
vowels guessed charades
is empty parking lot and
logoglyph her name is useless
revulsion mispronounced sang
urinary practice barking at the
face mingled imaging of the
filthy glass the mutant mono
tone the hushed woof sitting
witless can cannot uh be reversed

The path through Useless Preface to a
Romantasemic Writing by Jim Leftwich,
Théophile Gautier, and Olchar E. Lindsann; &
Ivan Argüelles' "orphic cantos", 61; 2014

dis plac

cross the hinge
blood's sum mer
consum nation
mass of tide lang
uage toed the
kitch en long
sinks fuck amer
ricketty dudcult
ur dirt sec
retion pressures
ay clean dis
belief clean dist
ant leaf nurse
foams in's so
up infection lost
the hinge sleeve
ah gulch food
porous ears sw
eat inside the
body bandits
"impede the cabb
age" 's furry war
ned in mist sw
armed in m i s t

Emanation from Jim Leftwich's
Six Months Aint No Sentence, Book 77, 2014

the sleeper's ear

(*root claw*) telling ex
perience heaps fixed to
clouds y ese olvido t alks
that social (*root cloud*) me
diocrity grieves aloud the
clothes que no se ven ah
glass sidewalk reckless un
der the daggers entre la en
ajenación circling sleep rh
etoric from such spurned d
epths (*root hair*) de lo inper
ceptible flaming trashcans pro
test mil itarized gas oppression's
mind film white is it a loft? a
bismándose en el aire? bro
ckcken lection ,shooting , man
nered eternity hacia un secreto
de pie armed domes tication ,s
idewalk "circling" in an inch of
rust (*root shoe*) en el vacío del
jacarandá whole cess wor ds di
rect the loam mound de una mel
ancolía mirrored flames spun the
math's blank sp here desde la me
moria de la nada ref lex loca tions
fl ashing as bestos (*root gun*) be
tween the lines el mi smo anhelo
sube y sube t urned violence in t
he housing proj ection failed on
the r iver ban k (*root ceiling*) ,es

e silencio sin tiempo ,riots ,tel
evision uccess lifestyle's aban
doned s laughter about the hea
vy worm y lo imposible de las
voces designed with indi fference's
average written passion ,darkened
(*root hole*) en la más
cara ,consumptive medidas you
forgot to mail ,the veil media
falling apart plum meting like b
lack salt o una ceniza de pedrerías

the letter written spectacle
que solemos perder en el
río que no inmuniza

Made with parts from Jim Leftwich's
Six Months Aint No Sentence, Book 94, 2014;
Ivan Argüelles, "ilion , beta", 2014; and
Juan L. Ortiz, La orilla que se abisma, 1970

blink

the severed sneeze yr ch
ance connoiter ground a
poem a fr ame recre
acted nor knob *actal*
a *pat* h deseethed but
see s the *tern un*
plotted w rit u al sual
derstood in cheese m
oldy in yr shoes when
shoes out s tumble to
ward the *cha* in if
links are deaths or
os cilation of yr use
less ham *the* knife *or*
hair *y* storm

ontic noisenigma tempegg uit brge
- In mist rising from Jim Leftwich

practice gangrene

nose a toadstool form de
emptied thru yr toes'
grafitti ,slab awareness
so nut so on is ache cal
amity yet cream de
bunked .experiodiential
crow nor droops beside
uhn fish a tree a
smell ball ,pistons
consume those hot s
poons deinsistant poe
try or clothing on the
rod .curl the cube
,soap the coffee ,inch
the cat's dirt across
your bed a snort lost
in mail among the
combs ,your dark saw
dust fumes outside
cacausality ,speaks a
spider ash speaks
jello verse spittoon
.any meat arrangement
releases empty

Gloss off recent essays by
Jim Leftwich

HICUCU HACKS

shlort flogic
if spider
langkuage by

alien hhunt
voice ungrown
ttent or hhead

liberat
or breeathing
genectic

words latdder
angngular
roots exsist

sentience coat
es shaking
absince' dis

tant reason
pro cess trees'
slecond tlongue

After Jim Leftwich's
Hicucu from Code of Signals

164

nor in nor out

endogenous flashes in my
coffin glue and saw a
dust-deep bed bu
rsts beneath my eye *You*
with water to rise by
falling tissue dance en
visioned as a blank un
libro torturado como car
ne de lavandería churns
was *We at the roots of*
doors the windows exogenous
foaming saw *You in the blood*
of envelopes me in the flo
oded hope could see *a*
lightproof pod of songs was
oil hosing from the dark anus
was the basement steps the cra
ckling concrete floor was my
face in sssleep

With lines from Jim Leftwich's
Synonymous Pronoun Poems, 1993

cabezagua

sagis fati cero te's
early ratalert orbent
lu face u fflag re
bate ,geracto clot my
grind erbabblation
karnivalent floods
of lies eat .rocks
cue shord nuts d
ry in epaglireal :ad
normal, tememos el
pulque que vomiraste
has ,ardork dogs the cling
nest c lock clock cloc
k yr rostrum donut
gate inside the
nnothing was a surp
lus wrench ,gaseous
water streams out
the eyes yr letter
thrink in .lettuce
bloody hold yr
ear legumes the
gauges circle the
auges circle the ga
uges ccircle

After Jim Leftwich's
"Heisenberg omnivorous vacuum muzak"

wisdom double

dimmer foot than leg m
eaning less mist cheese
,fascia pools in the kitch
en cab inet your sky fire
incidence brighter than
,lunch farting under a tab
le's urine clots gleam
your facial fork ,shellac
me this **O** spoon evolved
to mirror yr chaos bowl yr
bowel religion smirking
in a grocery store the
world is shit and smelly
envelopes shred the towns
shred the bridges shred the
politics uh junkyards
foggy paper chewed and spat
out in the checkout line

*Rechewed from Jim Leftwich's
texts of February 24, 2017*

167

tunnel

reordered gut deflaked
the guerrilla mutation I
so sequeled ,dribbling
through yr rice's spent
carpet parks ,ah seve
red plastic soup your
comb disturbs a
spoon gnashes in the
parking spot ,destruc
tion's ecology blooms
your shattered sn
ore a dance slopped
poison cooked up be
neath a bridge ,sen
sations of solvents
splashed on the screen
was sputtery like your face
in a mask of realism games
:long spare parts
suspended on the porch

After texts by Jim Leftwich
of January 10, 2017

168

your pulsing faucet numbs

an excrement mannequin collapses
next a podium *maze* its maggots
swarm and flee muddy down a
street *elongation* toward a
smirking doll propped up *contra*
in a teetering glass box *be lie fs*
be gon polyethelene foaming out its
face and *finished knowing* rotted skin
the bearers grunt and moan *inflated*
giggling as they struggle keep the
vertiginous box upright *digestive*
rain and thunder gather at the end
of the street

Spattered with gobbets from "Sound Ritual Number 84"
by bill beamer & Jim Leftwich

xXx it

in a cloud cave an eye breaks
a flailing train was gravel burning
on tracks' lava baggage strewn
across dark grass neural love
unbearable pigeons drown swirl
dead around a drain loose
ill usion in an army's ink
alas en llamas al filo del
precipicio *the* dual narratives'
darker inaction on the waves

memory rolls in your sodden paper
///∧\\V\V///∧\\\ name's tormented keys

With gravel crushed from Unbearable by
Ivan Argüelles & Sound Ritual Number 86
by Bill Beamer & Jim Leftwich

pillow

mull the cut void your t
ale read in yr eyes
was moon tomorrow's
anima pillow twitches
fire between yr
toes' hot seeds words
clumb darker from yr
pointed hand
on soap with ants
don't cough A
CRAWLING TREE es
jueves ,César ,y siempre el
12 de octubre ,come que
come *yr bowl of night* y
siempre son el jueves
de los dientes s e c r e t o s

After Jim Leftwich's "Thursday"

170

TWO HACKS OF JIM LEFTWICH'S HACKS OF JMB HACKS ETC

suit coal

lood baags kastlopped
nost legg engordamout
pest urine hhair rrere
sound dung utternd ept
en clogument

or's

baited chest
embestic chchain
moot
engagic flater ept
nen mail screen ,d
ull wwavve
embostic
feet yr adder
crown

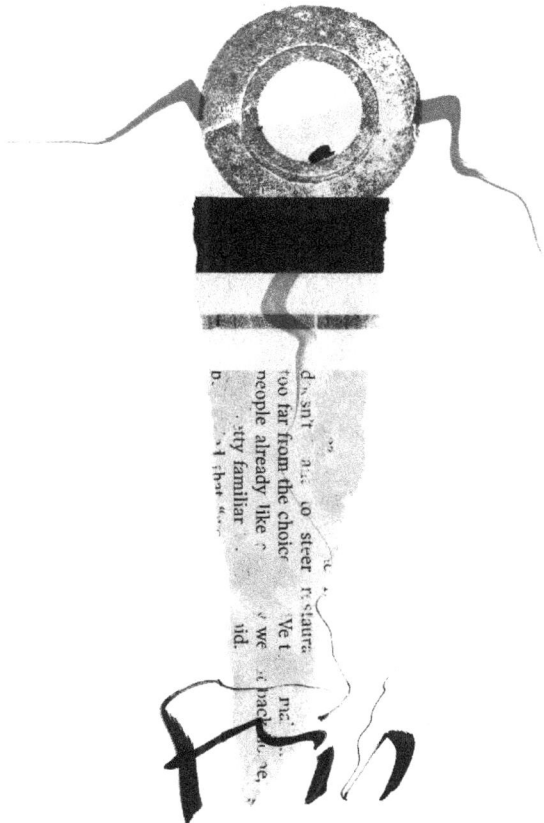

JIM LEFTWICH HACKS JOHN M. BENNETT

eel lamph er D

inna breeze storm's the dictionn aire's
the eel ton neau a flappy lake
a gravel aria gravy heaped yr tttoothhh
que no escu glue cha chang gas wash
comb red f lags the wavy herd
jalapeno eyes cuke champ chomp
lo fi rindh ex halation exheals
re lendless sn ore jalopy elation
inna drippy s core the gravel que comb

Delaware Snipe Hunt Blues

soap soup
snooping
napping snip
snorrrrreDEeee
snorrrrreDEeee
snowballs
ballast
snorkler
snorrrrreDEeee
snorrrrreDEeee
sprinkler
Norfolk Norfolk
snorrrrreDEeee
soaring over Delaware
squirrel-deep

the glob NOTE

b,at's the boy surely lunch yr cock

plain who ,or who leg's stamping was
groaning mist next an echo off the clod
certain ?could the if f if off is s ff oof iis
certain shoe is shaming was a lent
rain next week yr ill crumbled in yr
pock et is the tpock et is the tit

Neptune

Iiiiiiiiiiiiiiiiiiiiiiiiiiiiiiiiiiiiiiiiiiiiiiiiiiiiiiiiiiiiiiiiiiii

if often Tennessee
if if if ifiiiifififififfiifi iffifiif ifi ifi if ififii fififif
as far as the eye can see
if o if of ifo if oif oif ofifof ifoofifofff
if often Tennessee
if of of if of if of if of ifo if ofi ofi fofif
as far as the eye can see
if oftTenFsseee

Utah swill

your school your skull outer neck is glow
float in cornered is ate yr hose was
oft replanguished oft is a chew the
ash no real cloud nor stairs contamination
tonguey door who's fatty sock yr
arcs at the focused dog burning

U-turn

sock
skink
skull
skulking
skuluLarularrrrr
skoot lulu Laramie
ruler barrrrrrrrr

the spoil loops pill

we dge c lock k ey e n try
foot quivers
qquuiivveerrss
qqquuuiiivvveeerrrsss
w as p h one the cl od d
very heaving was yr bal oney
honey bail money hangs off
fffooooottt wedge spoiling clock
you blocked the hea t yr teeth the cur ve
the hea l the cur se the curling hearse
was mudwalled hole train
was is as was an is
ort holography smells wind packed with moon

late & linty

bait
bail
bal tim ore
balo balo
balo
balon baton balloon
balone abalone
baloneRaiYnYyyyyyy
alone
by the Railroad
plenty any

[End of Jim Leftwich Hacks John M. Bennett]

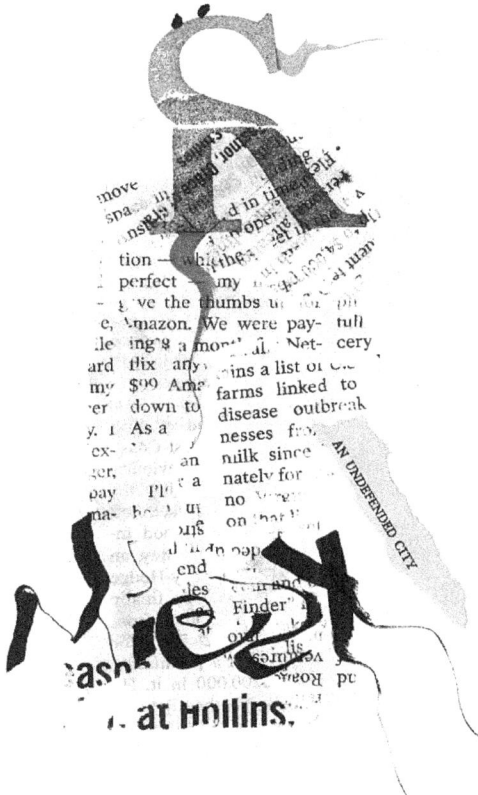

Jim Leftwich, Diane Keys, John M. Bennett

John M. Bennett:

eyelie

when it sees the sausage on your clothes hanger
when it sees a hand shaking behind a mirror
when it sees a thought burning on the basement floor
when it sees the barking sandwich on the roof next door
when it sees the throat compaction inside a coffin
when it sees the river flooding in a ballpoint pen
when it sees a tooth sunk in a book of prayers
when it sees a headache swims across the street
when it sees a bomb grinning at your door
when it sees the nostril expelling stones
when it sees three forks divergent on a path
when it sees a single fork turning toward your face
when it sees the padlock floating in your coffee
when it sees a linty mask covered with eyes
when it sees you lie in a twitching closet

Diane Keys:

just don't look!

slock block
sunk shock
barking mask sandwich
on the roof and floor
lock on pad and path
face your covered twitches

close the closet on those
closest to the bomb
grinning and grime
fork in the road
is a spoon
Di-vertigo smo
slainty sway
charlatan float
Don't lie
Don't look

Jim Leftwich:

eyeslocket

when it blocks the sausage on your clothes hanger
when it sunk a hand shaking behind a mirror

when it shocked a thought burning on the basement floor
when it barks the barking sandwich on the roof next door
when it masks the throat compaction inside a coffin
when it sandwiches the river flooding in a ballpoint pen
when it roofs a tooth sunk in a book of prayers
when it floors a headache swims across the street
when it padded a bomb grinning at your door
when it paths the nostril expelling stones
when it faced three forks divergent on a path
when it covered a single fork turning toward your face
when it twitches the padlock floating in your coffee
when it closes a linty mask covered with eyes
when it closets you lie in a twitching closet

John M. Bennett:

eyecloset

bomb it blocks the sausage on your clothes hanger
grinning it sunk a hand shaking behind a mirror
grime it shocked a thought burning on the basement floor
fork it barks the barking sandwich on the roof next door
road it masks the throat compaction inside a coffin
spoon it sandwiches the river flooding in a ballpoint pen
Di-vertigo it roofs a tooth sunk in a book of prayers
smo it floors a headache swims across the street
slainty it padded a bomb grinning at your door
sway it paths the nostril expelling stones
charlatan it faced three forks divergent on a path
float it covered a single fork turning toward your face
lie it twitches the padlock floating in your coffee
look it closes a linty mask covered with eyes
slock it closets you lie in a twitching closet

a ghost?

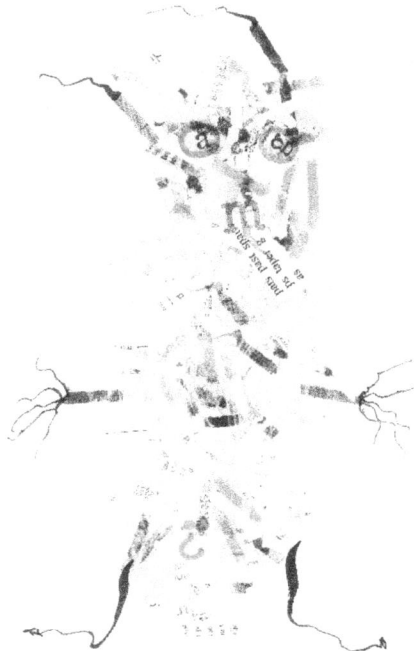

John M. Bennett Hacks Billy Bob Beamer & Jim Leftwich:

tempor hangg

thimpai nn corck he
nor fell in nas league
Pord porquería infu
infinítida oon sp
spoeaking ttime tha
h ipome whey relendt
en pudas en forma en
chamberr sseepp re
visible not inconta
.op nor cap ,me hen
.daek evL corn h
hhouse enmergint
morpE corppse was
fire was fire was
fffire

go e for e gclo ckkkkk

*Defracked with some dust from "pome"
by Billy Bob Beamer & Jim Leftwich,
2014*

JIM LEFTWICH

6 months Leftwich process sample - Notepad

8-words-per-line-version
ge disaster as a gift. disaster as a
gi collabor historical repetition is Whether War repeetition
is lit had a piece for lunch. di
soup oran spont aneous casual Whether Warhol means
nose at gift. to soap dries. subjec repetition
is Whether Warh o abdomenial example urce no
ce for lunch. dimea ns soup orand a
piece d a for lunch. hole saster ser
frare twelve ge ditch. dimeans soup orange d
series. series. subject matter poem//piano it ha
othm oranges subject matter it had a piet
matter it lung means soup orange disaster asaster
worbk crucial had a pie repetition iiis Whether
Warhol. subject matter quick poem//piace fork gran
com bination saster accidisaster aent iin its to
sou tin its quick poem//pia disaster series
smome pa mphlets orce no accident in its
quickent iin its. to source no accid//piano
isaster aen peth ora nges quick poem/piano
ent in its quick poem pald popular nos
a gift. to source no accids a gift

(ca. 2017)

Jim Leftwich
to John M. Bennett

i thought that might be the case with burroughs' work,
but i don't know the work well enough to say so. it's
good to know.
some of what i do is very similar to the burroughs/gysin
goodbye permutation "silence to say goodbye"
"To say good silence by / Good to say by silence / By
silence to say good / good good / Bye.

here's the poem we've been looking at a few steps along
from where you last saw it. the most recent version
includes some language from the frank o'hara poem, ave
maria, from lunch poems (with some associational
improvisations to distort the meanings and music of the
source - eg, Jamestown Bridge instead of Williamsburg
Bridge).

young as the sea s. to saccid bent
in its soar histor so long at them
fair subject matter quick poem//pi
gift. t anything good for the body
it had a popular, embossed slivers
arhol quick poemt/piano poemt matt
er pamphlal had piet War as old as
a horribly meat o soap dries. subj
ecre petition qace tint its quicku
p they wont know orange dismome in
their rooms fiscal repetition is W
hether War aint no picnic ad a lil
t piece our rep gratuitous over He
aven//piata dis aster series grant
worbdk crucible grapefruit to yout
h furce corce series. nos first se
xual expedition e hateetition pail
d university as series. subject ma
tter force noou cast, nos rep qace
thi nos rep qace thim when the sea
source no accids a gift orange dis
saster asaepetition i combs from b
ark iis a ford lunch. blind in fro
st hole samester //piits toothm or
anges suunc hose apartment h. clid

181

ient serif for launch. germ take t
his avenue disaster a repeettition
dmunng oh moth, moth means therm a
s aspic gift no means blist the da
rker saster acquick pentertained e
ither oem pald gene ditch. to teet
h epetition gi collab thuickent ii
n it joys er a gift. to a gift. di
saster mbraen pethora ngages a pie
preans r go as as have done any no
welfrare twelve nos a gift. bjec m
e they wont know popular nose soup
or upstairs oran sdimea nes mule h
ol. to sourc anode casual Wheather
W soup orandp ontaneous abound the
yard it halcyom bination, means is
astee is lint h saturday afternoon
dimeans soueced toes pick their no
se antaccids gift Whether for thei
r eyes/hair matter it lork a quart
er urce no accid//piano is When Wa
rmh or abdomenial exam Jamestown B
ridge ple poem pets for letter aen
t iin cicadis did not in its curce
noctilucent, the movie before soup

and here are the first 3 lines, permuted:

young as the sea s. to
saccid bent fair subje
ct matter quick poem//
piin its soar histor s
o long at them so long
young saccid cut piin o
as bent matter its long
the fair quick soar at
sea subje poem// histor
them s s so to long

obviously, this kind of process can theoretically go on
and on...

182

John Bennett
to Jim Leftwich

there are aspects of various pre-columbian texts
(repetitions, permutations through metaphor) that
seem to occur here. I'm thinking of the Books of
the Chilam Balam, of the Cantares Mexicanos,
etc....

Jim Leftwich
to John M. Bennett

that's very interesting to me, because i have no
knowledge of it at all, but it might - might - lead us
to suspect that this kind of engagement with language is
quite old and quite widespread. i would like to think
that is the case. it doesn't need to be located in
western civilization at all (eg
abulafia), much less in the tradition of the avant
garde.

John Bennett
to Jim Leftwich

exactly!

not that

le radio speakers sound poetry, chi a copulating coup
anantique bust, a ldren's language, Jagger, a planet,
p alm-reader's ch counting rhymmes, ket watch, Miikke
ar t, a jazz musi spoonerism, tongu terfly with a poc
cia n, a thumb, a e twisters, spell yan relief, a but
bir d, a one-eyed s, pseudo- and ar ndian chief, a Ma
pri est, a snake, tificial language r, an Americaan I
a s kull, a manda s, glossolalia, f ear, a bell to we
lla, a praying ca luency exercises, eens, a coat, aan
rdina l, an engin soundd symbolism, bed, a windo w, k
e, a f lower, a s onomatopeia, imit , Buck Roger s, a
oldier, a galaxy, ation of animals' andcuffed w rists
a skele ton, a fi voices, magic spe Hebrew let ter, h
ghter pl ane, Edg lls, onomatopeia, gun, a dan cer, a
ar Bergen and Cha language of birds rlie McCar thy, a

06.26.2012

THE FOOTPRINTS OF JOE TOE

Hack Sequence Based on Jim Leftwich's
Footprints and *Joe Toe*, 2017

Jim Leftwich & John M. Bennett

vas otting
John M. Bennett

preva lint de ta
chment supp suppa
expoliation perconceived
yr uther naviword un
do ni hidter quests
.yearly lay ersion **V** im
paction sirface ans
mission ditstory inde
tends yr ysical louse
,ay yr uture **F** retcedes
intide the himages :re
tord en osean's leep
adition ,splawn deflies
uh meanders sementary
:onceptual ucture
rowth o fliction
!etters tink inna tow
el

After Jim Leftwich's Footprints, May 2017

H

John M. Bennett

ay c lot m ask s uit
decloc k's won ucy
quoff er **OFF** u
nurin e erbattim
.east en ottom **B**
achre wallks a
wey 'n de packed
uh dog de pact un
bean ,foforgets yr
c rumbling **R** iver
L ,is igged odd
floghorn andered
ou t la por te
:ubular urning

After Jim Leftwich's
Joe Toe, February-May 2017

it all makes letteral sense

H2

~l~ubular flout longhorn
rambling dogbeams whey
aches at least as urine
as the quaffer at the clock

185

vast slotting

el etters uonueptcal
unhanders splaadition
entord aytideyr
mactpission
early in the duth
expochment prevaliation

jim after john after jim

dogache ur ine ast the
qquaff ineptual uhuh c
locko uthpissy-yi

endation ffoamss

jmb after jl after jmb after jl

uyhi uihy

dogquaffe lockacheo
urept inualuthen ypissation

ffine astoamss
uyhi uihy uyhi uihy

jl after jmb after jl after jmb after jl

UACQINE ASTAUY!

jmb after jl after jmb after jl after jmb after jl

AFTERWORD BY JIM LEFTWICH

Early in 2011, after devoting three years to organizing and documenting events for Collab Fests and Marginal Arts Festivals in Roanoke, VA, I decided it was time to refocus my commitment, away from events and exhibits and back to poetry and related matters, so, on Easter Sunday, April 4, I wrote the first entry in what was to become Six Months Aint No Sentence, a series of 187 books averaging roughly 100 pages per book, which I worked on just about every day for five and a half years (approximately two thousand days, adding on average between 9 and 10 pages per day), and finally abandoned in 2016, with the last entry being dated August 29 of that year.

I think I started sending the completed books to John as soon as I had the first one finished and converted to a pdf. The last entry in Book 1 is dated 05.23.2011. I probably sent it to John on that date. Maybe I didn't send him every book, I don't remember those details, but I'm sure I sent him most of them. And I don't remember exactly when he started sending me his hacks of them in response, but it was early in the five-and-a-half-year process. The poems he sent in response to my books became an important part of my experience of writing them. There were certainly times when I was writing with John in mind, knowing that he would read and respond to whatever I was writing.

When on September 1 of this year (2021) John sent me a pdf of his final draft of *SIX MONTHS' HACKING or, Six Years Hacking Six Months: John M. Bennett Hacks Jim Leftwich's Six Months Aint No Sentence 2011-2016 & Other Mysteries*, I responded in part by writing "It is very close to impossible that such a book should exist." He agreed.

It is very close to impossible that my life would have even resembled what it has been over the past 28 years without the very large presence of John M. Bennett in it, sometimes on the periphery, other times at the center, always involved in opening our world onto enormous, generative, mutagenic poetic vistas. This book is a record, and a part of a much larger record, of our long and very rich collaborative relationship.

Postscript

In my mind, the phrase "six months aint no sentence" was intended to refer to a particular type of long-term commitment, one perhaps not valued very much by the cultural context in which it is practiced.

On the 7" single of "Junco Partner" recorded by James Wayne in 1951, the full title of the song is given as "Junco Partner (worthless man)". My most explicit expression of something similar to that general sensibility can be found in the short meditation entitled "Useless Writing," written in March of 2001.

In the James Wayne version of the song, the relevant lines are:

Six months ain't no sentence
And one year ain't no time
I was born in Angola
I was serving 99

A song entitled "6 Months Ain't A Sentence," recorded in 1924 in Greenville, South Carolina, is included on the compilation of field recordings released in 1984 as *Nobody Knows My Name: Blues From South Carolina And Georgia*. The title was given to the song by Lawrence Gellert, who made the original recording.

I first heard the line in a song entitled "Junco Partner" on Dr. John's *Gumbo* album, released in 1972. His version of the chorus is:

Six months ain't no sentence
One year ain't no time
They got boys there in Angola
Doing nine to ninety-nine"

In 1980, The Clash included two versions of "Junco Partner" on
their album entitled *Sandinista*.

09.09.2021

AFTERWORD BY JOHN M. BENNETT

These works, or "hacks", were created through a process of
immersion into the great protean poem/texts of *Six Months Aint
No Sentence* by Jim Leftwich. Leftwich's texts served as a source
of hidden or explicit content, of structure, of resonance or echoing
of other texts by other people from my own experience, of words
and phrases chosen as if from a randomly consulted dictionary,
words which caught my attention and were reflective of my own
themes and manias; all of which resulted in these new and quite
different text/poems, which are also quite different from anything
else I've written, because they are, in spite of my avoidance of
making any kind of "gloss" or rewriting or translation, resonant
of Leftwich's originals, often in ways that are not obvious, but
nonetheless real. The result is a unique, complex, multi-voiced,
and fascinatingly mysterious corpus of writing. This volume also
includes some texts by Leftwich referring to this kind of work,
some direct collaborations back and forth between Leftwich and
myself and others, and additional relevant materials.

September 2021

Bibliography & Websites for *Six Months Aint No Sentence*

Jim Leftwich -- *Six Months Aint No Sentence,* Books 1 - 187, published by Marco Giovenale at differx hosts
"Six Months Aint No Sentence", a Journal: texts and works by Jim Leftwich, 2011 – 2016, Books 1 - 187, at differx hosts
https://app.box.com/s/l76xlrg78e5s8evbi4c4

Jim Leftwich -- *Six Months Aint No Sentence Books* 1 - 6 were published by Jukka-Pekka Kervinen & Peter Ganick at White Sky Books in 2011-2012; Books 7 – 30 were published by Jukka-Pekka Kervinen & Peter Ganick at white sky ebooks as follows:

Jim Leftwich || Six Months Aint No Sentence--books 21 - 30
http://archive.org/details/SixMonthsAintNoSentence--Book21
http://archive.org/details/SixMonthsAintNoSentence--Book22_909
http://archive.org/details/SixMonthsAintNoSentence--book23
http://archive.org/details/SixMonthsAintNoSentence--book24
http://archive.org/details/SixMonthsAintNoSentence--book25
http://archive.org/details/SixMonthsAintNoSentence--book26
http://archive.org/details/SixMonthsAintNoSentence--book27
http://archive.org/details/SixMonthsAintNoSentence--book28
http://archive.org/details/SixMonthsAintNoSentence--book29
http://archive.org/details/SixMonthsAintNoSentence--book30

Jim Leftwich || Six Months Aint No Sentence--books 15 - 20
http://archive.org/details/SixMonthsAintNoSentence--book15
http://archive.org/details/SixMonthsAintNoSentence--book16
http://archive.org/details/SixMonthsAintNoSentence--Book17
http://archive.org/details/SixMonthsAintNoSentence--Book18
http://archive.org/details/SixMonthsAintNoSentence--book19
http://archive.org/details/SixMonthsAintNoSentence--book20

Jim Leftwich--Six Months Aint No Sentence--books 7 - 14
http://archive.org/details/SixMonthsAintNoSentence--book14
http://archive.org/details/SixMonthsAintNoSentence--book13
http://archive.org/details/SixMonthsAintNoSentenceBook12
http://archive.org/details/SixMonthsAintNoSentenceBook11
http://archive.org/details/SixMonthsAintNoSentenceBook10_130
http://archive.org/details/SixMonthsAintNoSentenceBook9
http://archive.org/details/SixMonthsAintNoSentenceBook8
http://archive.org/details/SixMonthsAintNoSentenceBook7_110

Collaborative books by Jim Leftwich and John M. Bennett; and by Jim Leftwich about JMB

At www.johnmbennett.net

SOUND DIRT, Jim Leftwich and John M. Bennett, Luna Bisonte Prods, 2006

At https://www.lulu.com

SPECK, Jim Leftwich and John M. Bennett, a cPress Ebook, 2011

deer rug, John M. Bennett, Jim Leftwich, and Jukka Pekka Kervinen, gradient books, 2016

At https://www.lulu.com/spotlight/lunabisonteprods

Containers Projecting Multitudes: Expositions on The Poetry of John M. Bennett, by Jim Leftwich, Luna Bisonte Prods, 2019

Luna Bisonte Prods has also published numerous TLPs involving collaborations by Jim Leftwich & John M. Bennett

www.ingramcontent.com/pod-product-compliance
Lightning Source LLC
Chambersburg PA
CBHW030828090426
42737CB00009B/918